Closing the Education Gap

Benefits and Costs

Georges Vernez
Richard A. Krop
C. Peter Rydell

Center for Research on Immigration Policy • RAND Education

The research described in this report was conducted in RAND's Center for Research on Immigration Policy. It was supported by grants from The Andrew W. Mellon Foundation and by The William and Flora Hewlett Foundation.

Library of Congress Cataloging-in-Publication Data

Vernez, Georges.
    Closing the education gap : benefits and costs / Georges Vernez, Richard A. Krop, C. Peter Rydell.
        p.   cm.
    "Prepared by RAND Education."
    "MR-1036-EDU."
    Includes bibliographical references (p.).
    ISBN 0-8330-2748-4
    1. Educational equalization—United States. 2. Minorities—Education—Economic aspects—United States. I. Krop, Richard A., 1962-   . II. Rydell, C. Peter. III. Title.
LC213.2.V47   1999
379.2 ' 6 ' 0973—dc21   99-23519
                                              CIP

Building on more than 25 years of research and evaluation work, RAND Education has as its mission the improvement of educational policy and practice in formal and informal settings from early childhood on. RAND is a nonprofit institution that helps improve policy and decisionmaking through research and analysis. RAND® is a registered trademark. RAND's publications do not necessarily reflect the opinions or policies of its research sponsors.

Published 1999 by RAND
1700 Main Street, P.O. Box 2138, Santa Monica, CA 90407-2138
1333 H St., N.W., Washington, D.C. 20005-4707
RAND URL: http://www.rand.org/
To order RAND documents or to obtain additional information, contact Distribution Services: Telephone: (310) 451-7002; Fax: (310) 451-6915; Internet: order@rand.org

To the memory of C. Peter Rydell

Education, more than ever, is key to a person's lifetime economic prospects as well as to making the most of one's talent and interests in a world that is rapidly changing both economically and politically. Indeed, as the economic returns to a postsecondary education have increased, those associated with the lack of such an education have diminished, contributing to an increase in economic disparities not only in American society, but throughout the world. At the same time, changes in technology and the growing availability of information are placing a premium on people's ability to process information in making everyday work and life decisions. Those who develop a mastery of the new information media and can apply them in everyday decisions will have an advantage over those who do not. Finally, the relationships between nations and, within nations, between governments and civil society are also growing more complex, and perhaps more democratic. Again, those who gain an understanding of these changing relationships and of the opportunities they offer will have an advantage over those who do not.

Equality of opportunity in education for all ethnic groups in the United States is a goal that remains to be met. Over the years, little progress has been made in closing the gap in college-going and college completion between blacks and Hispanics, on the one hand, and non-Hispanic whites and Asians, on the other. Rapid changes in the ethnic composition of the nation's population should make narrowing this gap ever more pressing. As a result of growing immigration since the mid-1960s, the fastest growing segment of the U.S. population is Hispanic, a group that, compared to others, is currently experiencing a significant lag in educational attainment. By year

2015, a majority of those entering the labor force for the first time are expected to be Hispanics (48 percent) and blacks (18 percent). In high immigration states such as California, these minority groups will constitute an even larger share of new entrants into the labor force.

We undertook this study to (1) promote a better understanding of what these changes in the population's ethnic composition mean for the nation's education of the labor force and for educational institutions and (2) explore the benefits and the costs associated with closing the gap in educational attainment, fully or partially, between ethnic groups. The costs of closing the gap would seemingly be high, but the public and societal benefits of doing so would be even higher.

This study is the first to estimate the implications for postsecondary educational institutions of closing the educational attainment gap. A significant by-product of this study is the simulation model that was developed, which states across the nation can use to assess the implications of closing the education gap for their educational institutions and for public spending on social and health programs.

This project was sponsored primarily by The Andrew W. Mellon Foundation. It also received support from The William and Flora Hewlett Foundation. The research was carried out in RAND Education's Center for Research on Immigration Policy. The results should be of interest to federal and state policymakers, education leaders, administrators of primary to graduate schools, and all those with an interest in furthering the goal of equal educational opportunity for all.

CONTENTS

FIGURES

TABLES

Ever increasing levels of immigration and the echo from the baby boomers are assuring that the size of the school- and college-age population will grow over the next two decades in excess of 15 percent. But immigration is not only contributing to the size of this population, it is also changing its ethnic composition, with most of the growth expected to take place among minority students, especially Hispanics and Asians. Projections are that, from 1990 to 2015, the share of Hispanics in the school- and college-age population will increase from 10 to 21 percent while that of Asians will increase from 3 to 6 percent. Projections for California are that more than half of this population will be Hispanic and another 14 percent will be Asian. The share of blacks is projected to remain constant while that of non-Hispanic whites will decrease significantly.

These projected changes in the size and composition of the school population present a particular challenge to policymakers for several reasons. First, the nation's educational institutions must educate this increasingly larger and more diverse population at the same time as public support for education has softened. Second, Hispanics, the fastest growing minority, are significantly lagging other ethnic groups in educational attainment, most particularly in college-going and college completion. And third, long-term structural shifts in the U.S. economy are making education in general, and postsecondary education in particular, necessary for anyone who wants to compete in today's labor market and command a living wage.

To improve policymakers' ability to make informed public education choices, this study explores the implications these trends have for the quality of the future labor force and for public social expenditures. It also examines the educational costs and social benefits of educational and immigration policy alternatives designed to close the gap in educational attainment between non-Hispanic whites and the lagging minorities, primarily Hispanics and blacks.

We developed a systemic and dynamic model of the flows of the U.S. population through the U.S. primary, secondary, and postsecondary education systems to support our analyses. This RAND Education Simulation Model keeps track of the entire U.S. population. The inflows to the population are births and immigration; the outflows are deaths and outmigration. The nation is divided into two regions: California and the rest of the nation. Migration flows between the two regions are recognized, as are the separate immigration flows into each region. In the model, the state region could be any state. We chose to model California because it has the largest immigrant and minority—mainly Hispanic—populations of all the states. The model simulates the detailed flows of students into and out of each high school grade and college level, starting with the 9th grade. Because the educational attainment and fertility rates of different groups in the population have historically varied, the model separately tracks 20 population groups differentiated by ethnicity, nativity (place of origin), and gender. For each year and each grade, the model projects the number of students in each group who remain in the grade for another year, the number who leave school, and the number who continue on to the next grade. It also projects the annual number of people who return to school at various levels after having been out of school. And, most important, the model projects the level of education achieved when people leave the educational system, student enrollment in terms of full-time equivalents (FTEs), and the costs of education. Then, using our estimates of the relationship between educational attainment and spending on public social programs, tax revenues, and income, the model projects the costs and benefits of changing the distribution of educational attainment.

This study is a first exploratory effort to develop and assess alternative long-term strategies designed to minimize the education gap. We address three major questions:

- What might the future educational attainment of the population be if the current immigration and school- and college-going patterns continue?

- What benefits and what costs are associated with closing, partially and fully, the educational gap between non-Hispanic whites, on one hand, and blacks and Hispanics, on the other?

- How sensitive to immigration policy is the distribution of educational attainment within the population?

In a subsequent effort, we hope to use the RAND Education Simulation Model and detailed information on existing programs and implemented strategies to assess their long-term cost-effectiveness for increasing the educational attainment of minorities.

From our current study, we conclude the following.

First, in spite of the rapid growth in the share of minorities in the nation's population, the educational attainment of the adult population age 25 or over will be higher in 2015 than it was in 1990. This finding reflects the dual dynamic process of (1) older, less-educated generations of people dying and being replaced in the labor force by better-educated new entrants (including minorities) and (2) the children, grandchildren, and so on of immigrants achieving increasingly higher levels of education. This pattern of higher educational attainment in 2015 than in 1990 cuts across all ethnic groups, including people of Mexican origin, other Hispanic origin, and Asian origin.

Nevertheless, unless further gains are made in the educational attainment of minorities, the share of college educated among future new entrants—age 25 to 29—into the labor force will decrease. Also, the educational gap between blacks and Hispanics, on the one hand, and Asians and non-Hispanic whites, on the other hand, will increase. Our projections are that this increase will be most particularly evident in California, where blacks and Hispanics will constitute an overwhelming majority (75 percent) of the state's high school dropouts while Asians and non-Hispanic whites will constitute an overwhelming majority (89 percent) of the state's college graduates.

Second, closing the educational gap for blacks and Hispanics would clearly pay for itself not only through the resulting long-term savings in income transfer and public social programs, but also through the resulting increased tax revenues and increased disposable income for the individuals involved. This is particularly the case in California, where nearly half of the student population today is Hispanic. Increasing educational attainment would, however, require sizable—up to one-third—increases in the capacity of (mainly) postsecondary educational institutions and, hence, significant dollar investments. One obstacle to getting this investment made is the fact that the spending of these dollars and the accrual of benefits from that spending do not overlap: the first is concentrated in the early years of a cohort, and the second takes place after education ends and is spread over an individual's lifetime. Our finding that the costs of closing the gap may be recouped within a decade or so—well within the lifetime of most of those called upon to make the investment—provides a strong argument that indeed the investment is in their self-interest as well.

Another obstacle to be overcome is that the incentive states have to invest in education may be less than optimal, most particularly for postsecondary education. We found that states can significantly alter the distribution of the educational attainment of their labor force through both internal and international migration. Hence, a state that does not produce the number of college graduates it needs can import them from another state or from another nation and incur no immediate cost. The other side of the coin is that a state that invests in producing many college graduates may not capture the full benefit of its investment. The size of this phenomenon is not insignificant and is a strong argument for the federal government to play a leading role in promoting and funding efforts to close the educational attainment gap for blacks and Hispanics.

In addition to requiring an increase in the capacity of the nation's education, increased educational attainment for blacks and Hispanics would require that programs designed to support and promote the educational persistence and achievement of these minorities be implemented on a much larger scale than is currently the case. We did not address this issue and the additional costs that such an expansion might require. We hope to do so in subsequent work.

Finally, we found that the pattern of immigration that has prevailed since the mid-1960s is a major contributor to the gap in educational attainment for certain ethnic groups. Changes in immigration policy that reduce the number of immigrants or limit the permanent entry of low-educated immigrants (those with less than 12 years of education) would do as much to reduce the gap in the share of the nation's high school graduates between Hispanics and other ethnic groups as would an equalization of high school graduation rates between Hispanics and non-Hispanic whites. However, changes in immigration policy would do nothing to close the education gap between blacks and non-Hispanic whites.

Another thing that changes in immigration policy—even a major decrease in the number of immigrants allowed into the United States—would not affect is the future ethnic composition of the population. Regardless of whether immigration continues at recent levels, the immigration that has taken place over the last few decades and the higher fertility rates of Hispanics and some Asians compared to other population groups assure that the shift in the ethnic composition of the nation's population will continue.

ACKNOWLEDGMENTS

We want to thank Stephanie Bell-Rose of The Andrew W. Mellon Foundation for providing both financial support and encouragement for this effort. She helped shape the research questions and saw the potential benefits of this kind of inquiry.

We also want to acknowledge our coauthor and colleague C. Peter Rydell, who passed away unexpectedly in October 1997. We are particularly grateful to Peter for his development and implementation of the RAND Education Simulation Model. Without him, this report would not be; we could do no less than dedicate it to his memory. Peter enriched our lives in many ways. His enthusiasm for public policy and his constant questioning of basic assumptions were contagious. His humor kept us going when we thought we would never get the model working. And his technical abilities in and love for spreadsheet modeling provided a new analytic tool, one we hope will be used by many others in the future. This is one of the many legacies he left us. We remember him as a most esteemed colleague and intellectual leader.

We also want to thank Lee Mizell, a graduate student at the RAND School for Public Policy. She rapidly learned how to work with the RAND Education Simulation Model and made some of the runs whose results are reported here.

Maryann Jacobi Gray at the University of California at Los Angeles and Robert Lempert at RAND reviewed a draft of this report. We thank them for making numerous organizational and substantive suggestions that contributed immensely to a better product. They are, however, not responsible for the report's conclusions and its shortcomings.

Finally, our thanks to Karla McAffee, who typed several drafts, including the draft of this final version, with good humor and professional efficiency.

Chapter One

INTRODUCTION

Three major trends are converging to make the education of the future generation of America's children particularly challenging. First, the nation's educational institutions must educate an increasingly larger and more diverse student population, a growing share of which is lagging behind the rest in educational attainment. Second, structural shifts in America's economy are making education in general, and postsecondary education in particular, necessary for anyone who wants to compete in today's labor market and command a living wage. And third, this increase in demand comes at a time of declining public budgetary support. The challenge is to be taken seriously, for these trends are neither recent nor merely cyclical. They are long-term trends that have been developing since the 1970s as a result of changes in the nation's immigration policy and of world-wide competitive pressures.

To improve the ability to make public education policy choices, this study explores the implications these trends have for the quality of the future labor force and for public social expenditures. It also examines the educational costs and social benefits of closing the gap in educational attainment between non-Hispanic whites and the lagging minorities, primarily blacks and Hispanics.

CHANGING DEMAND FOR EDUCATION

Several long-term trends are altering the national demand for education in terms of its size, composition, and geographical distribution. To illustrate the magnitude of these changes in demand, we have projected, to year 2015, the characteristics of the school- and college-age population by age, ethnic group, and immigration status using conservative birth, death, and immigration rate assumptions.[1]

Steadily growing immigration since the mid-1960s and the echo from the baby boomers are assuring that the size of the school- and college-age population (hereafter referred to collectively as the school-age population) will grow over the next two decades. Immigration is now adding more than 1 million to the nation's population every year. And these immigrants, mostly young, have a fertility rate that exceeds that of the native-born population. The number of persons 0 to 24 years old is expected to increase by 15 percent or more between 1990 and 2015 (Table 1.1). And the number of persons in the 15- to 17-year-old high school age cohort is expected to increase by 20 percent over this period of time.[2]

Hispanics are expected to account for the bulk of the increase in the school-age population between 1990 and 2015. We project that they will double in numbers and in share, with nearly half of this population being of Mexican origin (Table 1.2). The share of blacks in the school-age population will remain constant, but their numbers are expected to increase by about 3 million. We also project that Asians

Table 1.1

School-Age Population by Age, 1990–2015

Age	1990 (millions, actual)	2015 (millions, projected)	1990–2015 Growth (percent)
0–3	14.4	17.0	18.6
4–6	10.7	12.5	16.0
7–14	27.8	32.0	15.1
15–17	9.9	11.9	20.8
18–24	25.8	29.0	12.1
Total	88.6	102.4	15.5

SOURCE: U.S. Census of Population and projections by RAND.
NOTE: Numbers are rounded.

---

[1] We used the analytical model described in Chapter Three to make these projections. Our assumptions for birth, death, and immigration rates are discussed there.

[2] This increase in school-age population could be larger or smaller depending on changes in fertility rates and immigration policies.

Table 1.2

School-Age Population by Ethnicity, 1990–2015

Ethnic Group	1990 (millions, actual)	2015 (millions, projected)	1990–2015 Growth (percent)
Asian	2.8	6.3	124.1
Black	12.9	15.6	20.8
Hispanic	10.6	21.3	100.9
Non-Hispanic white	62.3	59.2	−5.1
Total	88.6	102.4	15.5

SOURCE: U.S. Census of Population and projections by RAND.
NOTE: Numbers are rounded.

will add some 3.5 million school-age persons, doubling their share. Asians are currently the fastest growing minority, but they will continue to be the smallest minority group in terms of numbers.

In contrast, the share of the non-Hispanic white population is expected to decrease from 70 percent in 1990 to 58 percent in 2015, and this group's absolute number is expected to decrease by 3 million.

Both the growth and the compositional shifts in the school-age population are expected to impact the educational institutions of states differently. Clearly, the high-immigration states of California, Florida, Illinois, New York, and Texas will be more affected than other states.

These projected changes in the size, composition, and geographic distribution of the school-age population are of particular concern because Hispanics—as a group—are lagging other groups in educational attainment, most particularly in college-going and college completion. At the very same time, most new jobs added by the economy are being filled by workers with at least some postsecondary education. For instance, from 1980 to 1997, the U.S. economy added 34 million new jobs filled by workers with at least some college, but it shed some 7 million jobs filled by high school dropouts (Vernez, 1999). The real earnings of workers who had only a high school degree or less have also been steadily declining. The nation may suffer if this increasingly large minority is not provided with the tools needed to succeed in this changing economy. The demand for public social services may increase as an increasingly larger underclass develops, and the nation's social and political cohesion may erode as income disparities between ethnic groups in the United States widen.

GAP IN EDUCATIONAL ATTAINMENT

Just how large is the gap in educational attainment between Hispanics and blacks and other ethnic groups? Table 1.3 offers part of the answer. It shows the share of each population group that had attained a specific level of education, from less than high school graduation to completion of a bachelor's degree, for the cohort age 25–29 in 1990. Because most immigrants have completed their schooling prior to coming to the United States, we distinguish between immigrants and native-borns. The latter have been mostly

Table 1.3

Percentage Distribution by Highest Educational Attainment, Age 25–29, 1990

Ethnicity/Nativity	Grade 12 or Less, No Degree	High School Degree	Some College or Associate Degree	Bachelor's Degree or More	Total
Asian					
Native-born	4.6	23.7	31.3	40.3	100.0
Immigrant	11.5	19.6	25.7	43.3	100.0
Black					
Native-born	16.7	42.7	29.9	10.7	100.0
Immigrant	12.3	32.7	36.6	18.4	100.0
Mexican					
Native-born	22.3	40.3	28.4	9.0	100.0
Immigrant	61.7	22.9	11.4	3.9	100.0
Other Hispanic					
Native-born	22.2	33.5	29.6	14.7	100.0
Immigrant	32.7	30.4	24.6	12.4	100.0
Non-Hispanic white					
Native-born	9.0	35.6	30.7	24.8	100.0
Immigrant	9.1	28.5	28.3	34.0	100.0
All					
Native-born	10.8	36.5	30.5	22.2	100.0
Immigrant	31.2	25.3	22.2	21.2	100.0

SOURCE: 1990 U.S. Census of Population.
NOTE: Row totals may not add to 100.0 because of rounding.

schooled in the United States and hence more accurately reflect the performance of the various ethnic groups in U.S. educational institutions. And because the majority of Hispanics in the United States are of Mexican origin, we show their educational attainment separately from that of other Hispanics, most of whom are originally from Central America.

Among native-borns, Mexicans[3] have the lowest level of educational achievement. They are more likely—one in every five—than any other group, including blacks and Other Hispanics, to drop out of high school. And they are the least likely of any group to complete a bachelor's degree. For instance, they are 2.5 times less likely to hold a bachelor's degree than are non-Hispanic whites, and 4 times less likely than are Asians.

Native-born Other Hispanics and blacks also have lower educational attainment than do native-born non-Hispanic whites and Asians. To illustrate, 56 percent of non-Hispanic whites and 72 percent of Asians in this group have had one or more years of postsecondary education, compared to 44 percent for Other Hispanics, 41 percent for blacks, and 37 percent for Mexicans.

Similar ethnic differences in educational attainment are evident among immigrants. Mexican and Other Hispanic immigrants—who account for one-half of all immigrants in the 25–29 age cohort—have significantly lower levels of education than any other group, including their native-born counterparts. By contrast, the levels of education of immigrants who are Asian, black, or non-Hispanic white exceed those of their native-born counterparts. For instance, black immigrants are almost twice as likely as native-born blacks to hold a bachelor's degree (see Vernez and Abrahamse, 1996).

Over time, the college-going and college-completion rates of all ethnic groups have increased. But the significant gap in college graduation between native-born non-Hispanic whites and Asians, on one hand, and native-born Hispanics and blacks, on the other, has not

---

[3]Throughout this report, we use *Mexican* to refer to people born in Mexico and people of Mexican origin born in the United States. We differentiate between these two groups by using the terms *immigrant* and *native-born*. We do similarly for blacks, using *immigrant* and *native-born* to indicate birth outside the United States vs. inside.

changed, in spite of a steady decline in the gap in high school graduation (Figure 1.1).

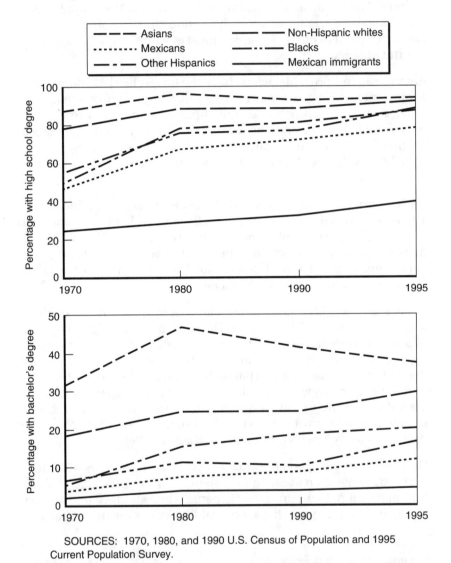

SOURCES: 1970, 1980, and 1990 U.S. Census of Population and 1995
Current Population Survey.

**Figure 1.1—Percentages of Different Ethnic Groups with a High School
Degree and with a Bachelor's Degree, Native-Borns Age 25–29, 1970–1995**

Indeed, the closing of the gap in high school graduation between Mexican, black, and non-Hispanic white native-borns appears to be one of the major educational achievements of the past two decades. From 1970 to 1995, this gap was halved from 31 percent to about 15 percent for Mexican native-borns and was closed for black native-borns. However, no relative gains have been made by either Hispanics or blacks in college completion over the past 25 years. Whereas this gap between Mexican and non-Hispanic white native-borns was 15 percentage points in 1970, it was even larger in 1995: 18 percentage points. For native-born blacks, the gap has remained constant over the past 25 years.

Among immigrants, the gap in educational attainment between non-Hispanic whites and Mexicans has remained extremely large (Figure 1.1). For high school graduates, this gap has remained constant over the past 25 years—exceeding 50 percentage points. For college graduates, the gap has significantly increased—from 17 to 26 percentage points between 1970 and 1995.

GOALS AND APPROACH

Because of the continuing differences in educational attainment between ethnic groups and the disproportionate growth of minorities in the school-age population, our study was designed to answer the following question:

> What would happen if the educational attainment[4] of blacks and Hispanics were increased and even equalized with that of non-Hispanic whites?

If blacks and Hispanics were to graduate from high school, go to college, and/or graduate from college at the same rate as native-born non-Hispanic whites:

---

[4]*Educational attainment,* the focus of this study, is measured by the number of years of schooling and/or the academic degrees obtained—e.g., high school degree, associate degree, bachelor's degree, Ph.D. It differs from *educational achievement,* which measures the knowledge acquired by students and the ability to use that knowledge. California's performance is relatively high on the first but relatively low on the second, at least as has been measured at the 4th, 8th, and 10th grade by the National Assessment Educational Program (NAEP).

- By how much would the postelementary education system have to expand to accommodate the resulting increased demand?

- How much more would education cost?

- What increase in the quality of the labor force would the additional education generate?

- What savings to government would the additional education generate, both by decreasing the demand for public social programs and by increasing tax revenues?

Answers to these questions would provide information about the consequences of policy choices regarding expanding or limiting access to postsecondary education, many of which are being debated in states around the nation. It would also provide information, heretofore unavailable, about the nature of the trade-offs between the short-term costs of upgrading the education of Hispanics and blacks now and the long-term societal costs of failing to do so.

To address these questions, we proceeded in three steps. Our first step was to estimate the relationship between educational attainment and public spending and revenues. It is well known that low education generally leads to low incomes and low lifetime earnings, which in turn increase dependency on social safety net programs such as Aid to Families with Dependent Children (AFDC), food stamps, and Medicaid. Conversely, higher levels of education lead to higher incomes, which in turn lead to higher tax revenues being available to pay for public programs. Other external benefits of education are reduced crime and hence reduced incarceration, and better health. We estimated the relationship between education and a comprehensive set of 14 programs associated with public welfare. We also estimated the relationship between levels of education and federal and state income tax, as well as sales and real estate tax payments. Our estimating procedures and findings are described in Chapter Two.

Our second step involved developing a systemic and dynamic model of the flows of the U.S. population through the nation's primary, secondary, and postsecondary education systems. The RAND Education Simulation Model, described in detail in Chapter Three, keeps track of the entire U.S. population. In any given year, the inflows into the population are births and immigration, and the outflows are death and outmigration. The model simulates the detailed flows of students into and out of each school and college grade starting with the 9th grade. For each year, the model projects the number of students who remain in a grade for another year, the number who leave school, and the number who continue on to the next grade. It also projects the annual number of people who return to school at various levels after having been out of school. And most important, it projects the level of education people have attained when they leave the educational system.

Because educational attainment has historically varied among different groups of the population, the model tracks 20 population groups separately, differentiated by ethnicity, nativity (immigration status), gender, and age. Among Hispanics, the model distinguishes between people of Mexican origin and "Other Hispanics" because the former is the largest group of Hispanics and has consistently lagged all other groups in terms of educational attainment. The model also separately tracks people born in the United States and people born elsewhere. The first group, the native-borns, receives all of its schooling in the United States, so its educational attainment depends entirely on the U.S. education system. The second group, the immigrants, primarily enters the United States as adults and by and large does not acquire additional education in the United States. For this group—which now contributes more than one-third to the nation's population growth—immigration policy is a more potent determinant of educational attainment than is education policy.

The value of the RAND Education Simulation Model goes beyond its use for modeling flows of the U.S. population through the education system. It can also be used for planning and to explore the educational consequences of potential changes in education and immigration policies. Moreover, it can be used to project into the next century the expected effect of population growth and compositional shifts on the demand for education and the expected distribution of educational attainment in the labor force. Because it has a state-specific module, it can also be used to analyze the impact of immigration on the education system of high-immigration states, such as California, New York, Florida, and Texas. Finally, it can also be used, as we used it, to estimate how various assumptions about changes in population growth and the distribution of educational attainment

across ethnic groups affect enrollment, education costs, public expenditures for social programs, and the distribution of educational
attainment.

In the last step, we used the findings from our first step and the
model developed in our second step to estimate the educational
costs and societal benefits associated with different goals that, if met,
could close the gap in educational attainment between non-Hispanic
whites and blacks and Hispanics. We considered maintenance of the
status quo—i.e., continuing the historical differentials in educational
attainment between these groups—and four alternative goals for al-
leviating those differentials: (1) equalizing high school graduation
rates, (2) equalizing college-going rates, (3) equalizing college-completion rates, and (4) equalizing overall educational attainment. For
each alternative, and over the lifetime of a specific cohort, we compared the distribution of its members' educational attainment, enrollment at each level of the education system, educational costs, the
costs of the public programs used, and the tax revenues collected.

As a nation, we could let the large differentials in educational attainment between the various ethnic groups in our society persist. But
even if we want to do no more than maintain the status quo, we will
have to increase the capacity of our education system in order to
meet the growing size of the school-age population. Failure to do so
will further increase the inequalities in education. Any effort to
reduce these inequalities will therefore require that the system's capacity be increased, which, of course, means that costs will increase.
However, a better-educated workforce may increase the nation's
competitiveness, and, most certainly, it will not only decrease public
expenditures for social welfare and health programs, but will also
increase tax revenues in the long term.

LIMITATIONS

This study was a first exploratory effort to quantify the costs and
benefits of meeting alternative goals aimed at closing the educational
attainment gap between ethnic groups. Hence, the reader should
take note of three major limitations to this study, the first of which
concerns the cost side of our estimates. We used average total costs

per full-time equivalent (FTE) student for each level of education.[5] To the extent that current educational institutions have excess capacity, our estimated costs will be higher than the actual costs of serving one additional student (the marginal cost). We chose to use average costs, however, because the combined increase in school population and college-going will most likely require increases in capacity, especially at the postsecondary level and especially in fast-growing states such as California, the state upon which this study focuses. Our estimates of costs also include both public and private costs. Clearly, there are trade-offs between these two types of costs, because increases or decreases in student fees and tuition affect public costs. This relative share is a policy variable. Arguably, increases in college-going for minorities—most of whom are in low-income families—will require public financing of most of their education, and implicitly this is our assumption. Our costs are total societal costs. In any event, readers should focus on the relative differences in costs—and benefits—of the alternative goals we consider, rather than on the absolute costs of any one alternative. Relative costs are less likely than absolute costs to be affected by the issues just raised.

A second limitation of our study concerns the savings in public ex-penditures. Although our analysis included the major public pro-grams (public assistance, Medicaid, Social Security, and Medicare), it did not include smaller programs such as public housing, rental as-sistance, state Supplemental Security Income (SSI) benefits, and job training. Hence, our estimates of spending on public programs may be low. Recent changes in federal program eligibility and benefits may also affect our projected estimates. In 1996, President Clinton signed into law the Personal Responsibility and Work Reconciliation Act (PRWORA) of 1996, also known as the Welfare Reform Act. It re-places the open-ended AFDC with a capped block grant giving states more flexibility in assisting needy families. It also limits the length of time benefits can be drawn to five cumulative years and limits access of legal immigrants to a broad range of federal programs—including

---

[5]FTE enrollment for institutions of higher education equals the enrollment of full-time students plus the full-time enrollment equivalent of part-time students. A student is enrolled full-time if she or he takes a course load equal to 75 percent or more of the normal full-time course load.

SSI, Medicaid, and food stamps—for the first five years of residence in the United States. These changes may lower public expenditures on social and health programs in the long term.

The third limitation concerns the target goals we considered. We estimated the key societal implications of reaching each of those goals and thus closing the gap in educational attainment across ethnic groups. But we did not address the fundamental question of how to meet the target goals. This question plays a part in our discussion in Chapter Seven.

In the future, we plan to expand our work to address in greater detail the cost issues raised above. We also plan to use the analytic framework described here to identify and assess the costs and benefits of alternative programmatic educational and social strategies designed to meet the goals considered here.

ORGANIZATION OF THE REPORT

Chapter Two presents our estimates of the relationship between educational attainment and government spending on public social programs, tax revenues, and individual income. Chapter Three outlines the structure of the RAND Education Simulation Model. This model, coupled with the estimates derived in Chapter Two, is then used to project the effects of changes in policies. Chapter Four projects, to year 2015, the size and educational attainment of the population under current school-going and immigration trends. Chapter Five assesses how closing the education gap, fully or partially, between non-Hispanic whites, on one hand, and blacks and Hispanics, on the other, could affect enrollment, costs of education, and public spending and savings. Chapter Six, in turn, compares how alternative changes in immigration policy might affect the context of education policy and the size of the task involved in closing the education gap. The last chapter briefly discusses the policy implications of our analyses and the proposed next steps.

Chapter Two

THE PUBLIC BENEFITS OF EDUCATION

The private returns to education receive considerable attention in both academic research and public policy discussion. The positive effect of education on individual wages and income is substantial and well documented, if not fully understood (Griliches, 1977; Ashenfelter and Krueger, 1992; Pascarella and Terenzini, 1991). Far less attention has been given to the public benefits of education (Stacey, 1998)—i.e., to the fact that education is a public good whose benefits accrue not only to the individual attending school, but to society as a whole. This public return to education provides a rationale for government support of education; in fact, most education, at both the K–12 and the postsecondary levels, is paid for by tax revenues. Whether the government should provide additional resources to meet the growing demands facing the nation's schools and colleges depends in large part on the value of the public returns to education.

These social, or external, benefits of education may exceed the private benefits—i.e., those enjoyed by the person who gets the education. For example, education leads to reduced crime, improved social cohesion, technological innovations, and intergenerational benefits (the benefits parents derive from their own education and transmit to their children). It also may affect public, as well as individual, health (Witte, 1997; Grossman and Benham, 1974; Grossman and Kaestner, 1997; Haveman and Wolfe, 1984; Psacharopoulos and Woodhall, 1985). And since the productivity of one worker often depends on that of others, education benefits the co-workers and employer of the individual who receives the education (Cohn, 1974). Both the amount and type of education received also may affect the overall performance of the economy (Haveman and Wolfe, 1984; Sturm, 1993).

Some have argued that education also has negative externalities associated with it. While workers may be more productive, they say, criminals may be more sophisticated. One problem facing developing countries in particular is the possible disruptive influences of unemployed graduates with frustrated expectations (Psacharopoulos and Woodhall, 1985).

An additional external benefit of education is its effect on the use of government programs, most particularly the means-tested programs such as welfare, food stamps, Medicaid, and other social redistributive programs. And education has an obvious effect on tax revenues: because income increases with educational attainment, and tax revenues increase with income, tax revenues should increase as educational attainment improves. By reducing the dependence on public assistance and other government programs and increasing tax revenues, the education of an individual may reduce the net cost of government programs to all members of society.

Few studies have systematically looked at the effect of education on public program use. Most studies look at only a few programs, and most do not explicitly account for the effect of education (Moffitt, 1992; Stacey, 1998). This relationship has to be understood and quantified, however, if the societal benefits of increasing the education of all or targeted groups of the population are to be fully assessed. This chapter presents a summary of our attempt to do just that. We first outline our conceptual and operational approach to estimating the relationship between educational attainment and public expenditures and revenues, and we then discuss our approach's limitations. Readers who are not technically inclined may skip this section, although they may benefit from reading the subsection titled "Limitations." We then present a section on our estimates of the effect education has on public expenditures for a set of 14 social programs, after which we give our estimates of the effect education has on individual income and tax revenues. Readers interested in a detailed discussion of our estimating techniques and findings should refer to Krop, 1998.

APPROACH

Conceptual Framework

Figure 2.1 illustrates our overall approach to estimating the benefits individuals receive from public programs. The arrows indicate the relationship among the variables. As can be seen, individual demographic characteristics, educational attainment, and parental background can affect program utilization and benefits both directly and through their effect on income. Parental background can also affect income and thus program use through its effect on educational attainment and family characteristics. Moreover, intergenerational effects may also play a part in program participation: an individual may be more likely to participate in a program if he or she grew up in a household that made use of the program (Rank and Cheng, 1995). And family characteristics—e.g., marital status and number of children—can affect eligibility and the amount of benefits received from some public assistance programs.

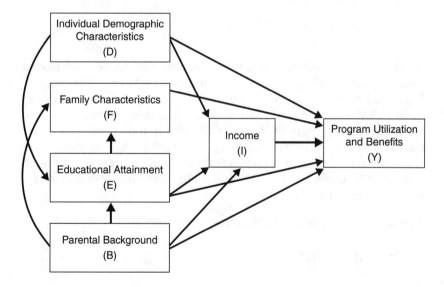

Figure 2.1—Program Utilization Model

Estimated Model

In Figure 2.1, parental background and individual demographic characteristics affect an individual's educational attainment. Although educational attainment is a choice variable, we treated it as an exogenous variable consistent with human capital theory (Willis, 1986), so what we actually estimated was the following reduced form model:

$$Y_{ij} = f(E_i, D_i, B_i)$$

where

Y_{ij} = benefits received (cost) from program j by person i.

E_i = education of person i defined as fewer than 12 years, 12 years, 13–15 years, or 16 years or more of education.

D_i = characteristics of individual i, including ethnicity, age, gender, and nativity.

B_i = parental characteristics.[1]

Because only a small share of the population receives benefits from a specific public social program (i.e., Medicaid or AFDC), this reduced form model was estimated in two steps according to a method developed at RAND (Duan et al., 1983). In the first step, the probability of receiving a public benefit in a year was estimated on a probit function of education and the individual's characteristics. In the second step, the annual benefit received from each program was estimated again as a function of the individual's characteristics using ordinary least squares (OLS) regression.

The individual characteristics in the model were specified as follows:

• Age and age-squared

---

[1]Because the Survey of Income and Program Participation (SIPP) does not provide data on parents' background, this variable was omitted in our estimates. However, we used data from the Panel Study of Income Dynamics (PSID) to assess the potential bias introduced by this omission. It was found to be small (Krop, 1998, Appendix C).

- A set of dummy variables indicating the level of educational attainment: less than high school graduate (LTHSG), some college (SC), or a bachelor's degree or more (BDP); high school graduates are the reference group

- Interaction between the age and educational attainment variables

- A set of ethnicity indicators: black non-Hispanic, Asian, Mexican, and Other Hispanic; non-Hispanic whites are the reference group

- A dummy variable indicating whether the person is native-born or an immigrant

- A dummy variable indicating whether the person was a student during 1991

Age was entered as a quadratic to allow the expected value of income from public programs to vary by age in a nonlinear fashion (Willis, 1986). Education was entered as a set of dummy variables to allow for a nonlinear effect of education on program income. The education variables were interacted with the age and age-squared terms to allow the effect of education on program income to vary by age. Therefore, the effect of education could diminish as the person grew further away from his or her formal schooling.

The analysis focused on per-person income from each program for all individuals age 18 or older. For programs targeting families, such as AFDC or food stamps, the benefit was evenly divided across all family adults covered by the program. For example, if a family receiving food stamps consisted of a husband, wife, and minor child, the value of the food stamps was divided equally between the husband and the wife. Money received by immigrants with native-born children was attributed to the immigrant parents. Income received by minor children was assigned to the adults in the family. Estimates of the income received by each group thus should not be biased.

Separate models were estimated for each of the following ten families of government programs:

- Federal and state unemployment insurance

- Federal Supplemental Security Income (SSI)

- Food programs, including food stamps and Special Supplemental Nutrition Program for Women, Infants, and Children (WIC)

- Low-income energy assistance

- Medicaid

- Medicare

- School breakfast and lunch programs

- Social Security, including railroad retirement

- Welfare, including Aid to Families with Dependent Children (AFDC), General Assistance, and other forms

- Criminal justice: jails and prisons

Separate estimates were made for men and women so as to be consistent with human capital models of labor market outcomes that allow for differences between men and women. (See, for example, Smith and Welch, 1986; Willis, 1986; Jaynes, 1990; Schoeni, McCarthy, and Vernez, 1995.) This approach enables us to see differences in education's effect on men's and women's program use. We would expect differences of this nature in the use of programs directed toward women, such as AFDC and WIC. The fact that women tend to earn less than men should also affect the benefits received from programs such as Social Security and unemployment compensation, whose benefits are tied to earnings.

Data

Data from the 1990 and 1991 panels of the Survey of Income and Program Participation (SIPP) were used to estimate the relationship between education and each of the programs listed above, except criminal justice.

The SIPP, administered by the U.S. Bureau of the Census, collects data for individuals over a 32-month period. The 1990 and 1991 panels overlap, providing data on approximately 114,000 people for 1991. Approximately 58,000 of these observations are for persons age 18 or older who were in the survey for all of 1991. The SIPP provides basic demographic data, including race and ethnicity, sex, age, immigration status, and educational attainment. It also provides monthly income from wages, savings and investments, business, and most major government support programs. In most cases, the SIPP indicates who uses each program each month and the amount of income received from each program. For Medicaid, Medicare, and school breakfasts and lunches, the SIPP indicates whether the individual is covered by the program but does not provide the value of the benefit. Appendix A discusses how we estimated the costs of these programs.

Data on the educational attainment of inmates of state prisons and local jails were derived from the 1991 Survey of Inmates of State Correctional Facilities from the U.S. Bureau of the Census and from the 1989 Survey of Local Jails, respectively. Both surveys provide basic demographic information on inmates, including ethnicity, age, gender, and educational attainment. While they do not provide information on immigration status, they do indicate whether a prisoner is a U.S. citizen. More details on these data files are provided in Appendix A.

Limitations

In interpreting the model's projections, the reader should keep in mind certain limitations, the first of which is that our estimates of the effect of education may be biased because our model does not include a measure of ability. There is, however, evidence that the bias introduced by excluding ability from the model is small and may even underestimate the returns to schooling (Griliches, 1977; Ashenfelter and Krueger, 1992).

Second, our measurement of social program usage reflects the state of the U.S. economy in 1991. While real gross domestic product (GDP) growth had recovered from the 1990 recession by the end of the first quarter of 1991, employment levels did not return to their peak until early 1993 (*Economic Report of the President*, 1996). Hence, our measure of program utilization reflects a period of slow economic growth. The bias introduced is not large, however. Table 2.1 compares the 1991 costs of public assistance and social programs and the average annual cost of these programs over the ten-year period from 1985 to 1995. The differences are generally less than 10 percent and go in both directions.

Table 2.1

Comparison of Costs of Public Assistance and Social Insurance Programs in 1991 and Average Annual Costs from 1985 to 1995

Program	Percent Difference Between 1991 Spending and 1985–1995 Average Spending
AFDC	2.6
Food stamps and WIC	4.7
Unemployment compensation	11.0
Federal SSI	–3.6
School breakfast and lunch	–6.0
Low Income Home Energy Assistance Program	–0.6
Social Security and railroad retirement	0.8
Medicare	–1.3
Medicaid	5.3

SOURCES: U.S. House of Representatives, 1996, and Congressional Budget Office, 1997.

NOTE: Unemployment includes state and federal benefits, including supplemental benefits. Medicaid includes both the federal and state shares.

EFFECT OF EDUCATIONAL ATTAINMENT ON EXPENDITURES FOR PUBLIC PROGRAMS

For each of the ten groups of programs, our estimated models yielded average program costs per person, at each of four levels of education, for each of 20 different population groups distinguished by gender; age; ethnicity (Asian, black, Mexican, Other Hispanic, and non-Hispanic white); and nativity, or immigration status (native-born vs. immigrant). Appendix B contains complete results for each program. Below, we illustrate and summarize our results, expressing all estimates of program costs per level of education in 1997 dollars.

Program Costs over a Person's Lifetime

Higher educational attainment leads to savings in governmental programs throughout a person's lifetime. Figure 2.2 shows the average per-person yearly costs of welfare payments for each of six groups of women from age 18 to 80. Several observations can be made from this figure.

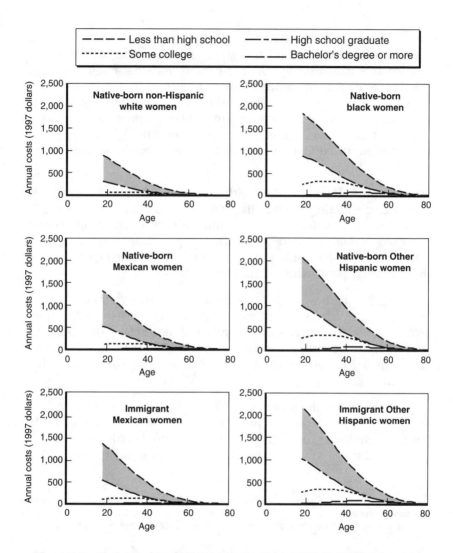

**Figure 2.2—Estimated Annual Per-Person Costs of Welfare for Selected
Groups of Women, by Level of Education and Age**

The average annual welfare cost per person declines with age, most
sharply for high school dropouts and then for high school graduates.
For persons with some college and college graduates, spending remains constant or even increases with age, albeit at a much lower

level of spending. The cost of welfare per person also drops sharply as educational attainment increases. For instance, for a non-Hispanic white woman of age 30, per-person welfare spending averages $623 for a high school dropout, about one-third that much for a high school graduate, and virtually nothing for a college graduate. The sharpest drop in costs (largest savings) occurs when educational attainment increases from high school dropout to high school graduate. Additional education yields increasingly smaller savings in welfare expenditures.[2]

Savings on welfare spending with increased education are cumulative over the lifetime of an individual. The shaded areas in Figure 2.2 show the savings that would accumulate over 32 years, on average, for each woman who graduated from high school instead of dropping out. The discounted 1997 value of those savings for a native-born non-Hispanic white woman would be $7,545.[3]

Figure 2.2 also shows that there are considerable variations in welfare spending across ethnic groups at the same level of education.[4] For instance, for native-born 30-year-old high school dropouts, annual welfare spending averages about $1,543 for a black woman, $973 for a Mexican woman, and $623 for a non-Hispanic white woman.

The result is that the same increase in educational attainment produces different average savings for different ethnic groups. An increase from high school dropout to high school graduate, for example, would result in an estimated $835 savings annually for a native-

---

[2]This pattern holds for all programs examined in this study except Social Security and Medicare, the two major social insurance programs for the elderly. For more details on the relationships between education and expenditures in these two programs, see Appendix C.

[3]Estimated at a 4 percent discount rate. We discuss the sensitivity of estimates to the choice of discount rate later in this chapter.

[4]We did not explore the factors that lead to these differences. Factors that have been found to be associated with such differences in the literature include participation rates, family size, and age of children. For immigrants, the factors also include legal vs. illegal status (DaVanzo et al., 1994; Halfon et al., 1997). Differences in the geographical concentrations of various ethnic groups may also lead to differences in spending, because states vary in the level of welfare benefits they provide.

born black woman aged 30, compared to $627 for her Mexican counterpart and $422 for her non-Hispanic white counterpart.

Finally, there is seemingly little difference in average welfare spending for native-borns vs. immigrants of the same educational attainment and ethnic group. For example, average annual spending for a 30-year-old native-born Mexican woman who has graduated from high school is $345, compared to $341 for her immigrant counterpart.

Variations in Medicaid Program Costs by Gender, Ethnicity, and Nativity

Figure 2.3 provides greater detail on variations in program spending by gender, ethnicity, and nativity. The bars in this figure represent the average per-person annual savings in Medicaid spending when a 30-year-old increases his/her education from high school dropout (the baseline) to high school graduate, some college, and college graduation.

In all cases, the greatest savings in Medicaid costs occur when education increases from high school dropout to high school graduate. As education increases, larger savings are estimated for blacks and Hispanics than for Asians and non-Hispanic whites. Within ethnic groups, immigration status has no sizable effect on public program use and costs.

There are, however, significant variations—on the order of magnitude 2 to 3—in Medicaid (as well as all other program) spending on women vs. men, the main reason for which is differences in eligibility requirements. Men are generally not eligible for AFDC,[5] and eligibility for other programs, including Medicaid and food stamps, is partly tied to AFDC eligibility. There are two exceptions to this pattern among the programs we considered. Men receive higher—almost three times higher—average unemployment benefits than do women, reflecting men's greater attachment to the labor force. And average expenditures for prisons and jails are typically ten times

---

[5]Exceptions are the small AFDC-U (unemployed fathers) program and the state-sponsored General Relief programs that some states have.

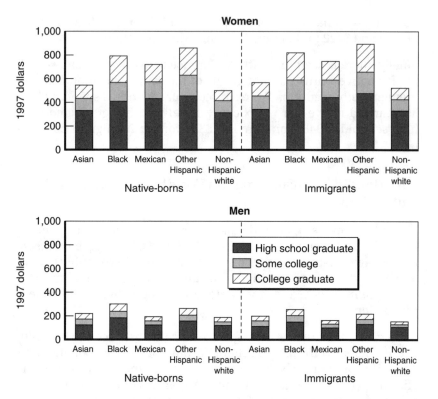

Figure 2.3—Annual Per-Person Savings in Medicaid with Increases in Education (Relative to High School Dropout) for a 30-Year-Old, by Gender, Ethnicity, and Nativity

higher for men than for women, reflecting the much higher probability of men committing crimes and being incarcerated.

Total Savings in Public Programs from Education

The pattern for welfare and Medicaid is repeated, with some exceptions (noted above), for most programs: the amount of public expenditure per person declines dramatically as educational attainment increases for all ages up to retirement age. Figure 2.4 shows the total annual savings in government spending on all ten groups of programs for 30-year-old women and men of different ethnic groups and nativity.

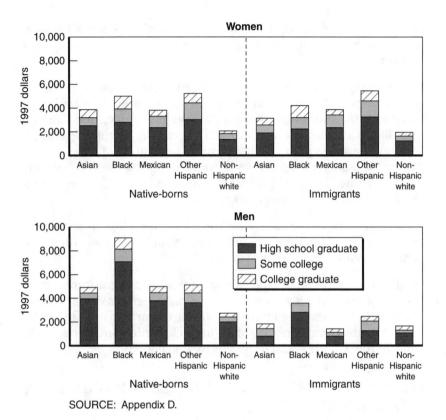

**Figure 2.4—Total Annual Per-Person Savings in Public Social Programs
with Increases in Education (Relative to High School Dropout) for a
30-Year-Old, by Education, Gender, Ethnicity, and Nativity**

Increases in educational attainment generate the largest savings for
native-born men, especially native-born black men. The bulk of the
savings for native-born men—ranging from 60 to 80 percent depending on ethnicity—is estimated to come from savings in prison and jail
spending. If the savings in criminal justice are not considered, the
savings in social programs for native-born men are typically lower
than those for native-born women. For example, a 30-year-old native-born black man who is helped to graduate from high school
would save $962 in this case, compared to $2,348 for a native-born
black woman of the same age. But when savings in criminal justice

are included, the differential is reversed: $7,064 in savings for a native-born black man, compared to $2,841 for a native-born black woman.

Lower savings in criminal justice are the main reason why the aggregate savings associated with higher education are lower for immigrant men than for native-born men. Again, when criminal justice spending is excluded, there are little differences in relative savings between these two groups. For instance, acquisition of a high school degree for a 30-year-old native-born Mexican man would generate $601 in savings in social programs, compared to $535 for an immigrant Mexican man of the same age.

Among women, increases in education lead to savings in social programs that are more than two times higher for blacks and Other Hispanics than for non-Hispanic whites.

Of all the groups considered in our analysis, immigrant men from Mexico generate the lowest savings in social programs with increases in education. These men have a high rate of participation in the labor force, are young, and are often undocumented and hence ineligible for most of the social programs we considered.

EFFECT OF EDUCATIONAL ATTAINMENT ON INCOME AND PUBLIC REVENUES

The effect of education on public spending is only part of the story. As is well documented, education leads to higher income and, in turn, to higher public revenues through federal and state taxes.

Education and Income

As we did for social programs, we used data from the SIPP to estimate the relationship between educational attainment and income for each of the 20 population groups considered. Because sample size was not adequate to produce an estimate of average income within each age and population group, we used an OLS model to produce estimates of income by age within each ethnic, gender, and nativity grouping.[6] To avoid double counting, and to estimate the private return to increased education, we subtracted estimated tax payments (see next subsection) from the estimates of pretransfer income.

Figure 2.5 compares, by ethnic group, the increases in after-tax average per-person income at age 30 as educational attainment increases. It shows that the relationship between increases in education and increases in average income is the reverse of that observed for increases in education and average spending on public social programs. An increase in education from some college to college graduation produces nearly 1.5 times as large a jump in income as an increase in education from high school dropout to high school graduate. And an increase from high school graduate to some college generates about the same change in income as an increase from high school dropout to high school graduate.

This pattern holds regardless of ethnic group, gender, or nativity. In absolute terms, the private return to education is larger for Asian and non-Hispanic whites than for any other ethnic group.[7]

Effect on Tax Revenues

As an individual's income tends to increase with educational attainment, so too do his/her taxes and contributions to social insurance programs, including Social Security and Medicare. Hence, we also estimated the relationship between educational attainment and three types of tax contributions: (1) federal payroll taxes for Social Security and Medicare; (2) federal income taxes; (3) state income, sales, and property taxes.

Social insurance contributions for Social Security and Medicare were estimated using the 1991 SIPP earnings data. Payroll taxes were estimated to be 15.3 percent of earnings up to $53,400 and 2.9 percent of earnings above that. Consistent with the fact that benefits under

---

[6]See Table B.11, Appendix B, for the detailed parameter estimates.

[7]Differences by ethnicity in choice of academic major, types of institutions in which students enroll, and other factors contribute to differences in income for similar educational attainment (Pascarella and Terenzini, 1991).

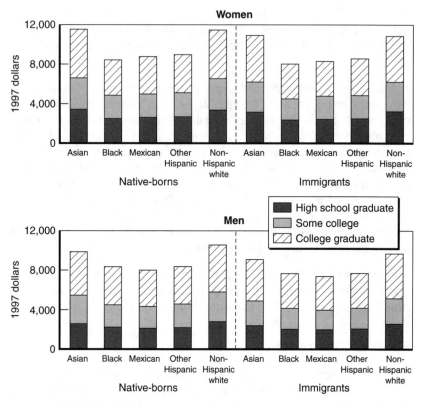

SOURCE: Appendix D.

Figure 2.5—Increases in Per-Person Disposable Income with Increases in Education (Relative to High School Dropout) for a 30-Year-Old, by Gender, Ethnicity, and Nativity

these programs are paid to both the worker and his/her spouse, we treated the contribution made by the individual worker as a payment divided between his-/herself and his/her spouse. To account for the fact that not everyone contributes to these programs, the estimated payroll tax payments were then entered as the dependent variable in a two-part model similar to the one described in our methodology section (see "Approach," above) to estimate the relationship between these taxes and educational attainment. Federal income and state taxes were estimated following a similar procedure, except that only a simple one-step linear OLS model was needed in this case.[8]

Figure 2.6 summarizes the total per-person increases in public revenues for women and men of different ethnicity and nativity. The increases in public revenues are substantial at every additional level

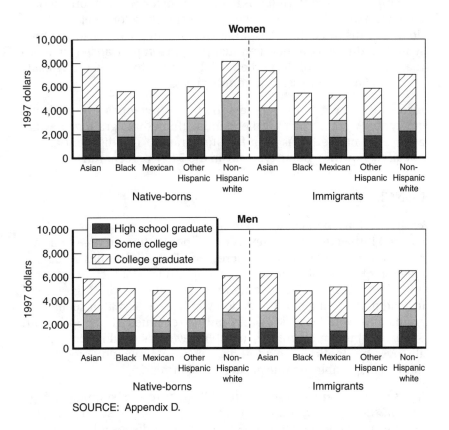

SOURCE: Appendix D.

Figure 2.6—Total Annual Per-Person Increase in Public Revenues with Increasing Education (Relative to High School Dropout) for a 30-Year-Old, by Gender, Ethnicity, and Nativity

---

[8]For federal income taxes, average rates by income class were obtained from the U.S. Department of the Treasury (1995). State tax rates were derived from Ettinger et al., 1996.

of education. The largest relative increase in public revenues occurs between those with some college and college graduates, reflecting the similarly disproportionate income growth for college graduates vs. those with some college. There are some differences between ethnic groups, with increases being 10 to 20 percent larger for non-Hispanic whites and Asians than for blacks, Mexicans, and Other Hispanics. This difference reflects the lower per-person income commanded by minorities even after accounting for level of education. For instance, non-Hispanic whites and Asians who are high school graduates command annual per-person pretransfer incomes that are in excess of 30 percent higher than those of their black, Mexican, and Other Hispanic counterparts.

Also, the increases in per-person public revenues are typically greater for women than for men; and within ethnic groups, they are greater for native-borns than for immigrants. The differentials are not large, however, being typically in the 5 to 7 percent range.

CONCLUSIONS

We have shown that large savings in public social programs would be realized if the educational levels of the population at large or a segment of the population were increased. Public revenues would increase largely by the same order of magnitude. For instance, for every native-born Mexican woman who graduates from high school instead of dropping out, the nation would save $2,438 in social programs and would add $1,843 in public revenues in her 30th year. Similar savings and increases in public revenues would accrue annually over her lifetime. In addition, this woman would enjoy $2,588 more in disposable income during her 30th year.

If this woman were to attend some college instead of stopping at high school, the result would be $956 more in program savings, $1,398 more in public revenues, and $2,401 more in disposable income at age 30. And graduating from college would add another $411 in program savings, $2,551 in public revenues, and $3,722 in disposable income.

Chapters Five and Six show how we used the relationships discussed here—those between educational attainment and savings on social program expenditures, and those between educational attainment and increases in both public revenues and private disposable income—to estimate the public and social benefits of partially or fully closing the gap in educational attainment between non-Hispanic whites and blacks and Hispanics.

Chapter Three

THE RAND EDUCATION SIMULATION MODEL

To assess the effects on costs and educational institutions of closing the gap in educational attainment between non-Hispanic whites, on one hand, and blacks and Hispanics, on the other, we developed a systemic and dynamic model of the flows of the U.S. population through the nation's primary, secondary, and postsecondary education systems. The RAND Education Simulation Model uses cohort-survival methodology to keep track of the entire U.S. population. In any given year, the inflows into the population are births and immigration, and the outflows are death and outmigration. The model simulates the detailed flows of students into and out of each school and college grade starting with the 9th grade. For each year, the model projects the number of students who remain in a grade for another year, the number who leave school, and the number who continue on to the next grade. It also projects the annual number of people who return to school at various levels after having been out of school. Most important of all, the model projects the level of education attained when people leave the educational system, FTE student enrollment, and the costs of education. Attainment is tracked at four levels: not a high school graduate, high school graduate, some college completed (including vocational education and associate degrees), and bachelor's degree or higher. Combined with our estimates of the relationship between educational attainment and spending on public social programs, tax revenues, and disposable income, the model projects the costs and benefits of changes in the distribution of educational attainment.

We first describe the key features of the RAND Education Simulation Model. We then outline the data used to operationalize the model, including the transition rates in and out of schools, immigration rates, and education costs. The third section here specifies the outputs of the model. We then conclude with a brief discussion of the model's uses and limitations. In subsequent chapters, the model is used to project the ethnic composition and distribution of educational attainment to year 2015 (Chapter Four), to assess the costs and benefits of closing the educational gap between non-Hispanic whites and minorities (Chapter Five), and to assess the effects that immigration policies have on the demand for U.S. education (Chapter Six).

STRUCTURE OF THE MODEL

Overview

The RAND Education Simulation Model uses cohort-survival methodology to keep track of the entire U.S. population (see Figure 3.1). The inflows to the population are births and immigration; the outflows are deaths and outmigration. The nation is divided into two regions: California and the rest of the nation. Migration flows between the two regions are recognized, as are the separate immigration flows into each region. In the model, the state region could be any state. We modeled California because, of all the states, it has the largest immigrant and minority—mainly Hispanic—populations.[1]

The model rigorously identifies whether a person is or is not in school during a given year. In particular, the migration flows between regions and the immigration flows from outside the country are all split into two parts. One part initially goes into the school system, and the other part initially goes into the out-of-school population account.

The model simulates the detailed flows of students into and out of each high school and college grade, starting with the 9th grade (Figure 3.2). Each year, for each grade, the model projects the number of students who remain in the grade for another year, the num-

---

[1] About one-third of the nation's immigrants and one-third of the nation's Hispanic population reside in California. In 1997, 25 percent of California's population was foreign-born, compared to about 19 percent in New York, 16 percent in Florida, and less than 11 percent in Texas. Also, one-fourth of California's population is Hispanic, compared to 26 percent in Texas, 13 percent in Florida, and 12 percent in New York.

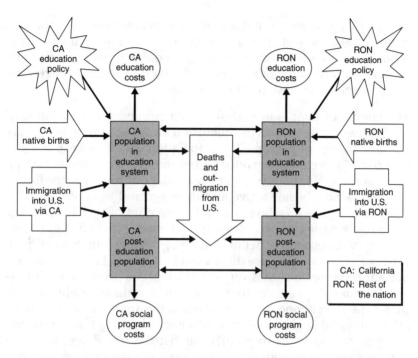

Figure 3.1—Annual Flows in the Education Simulation Model

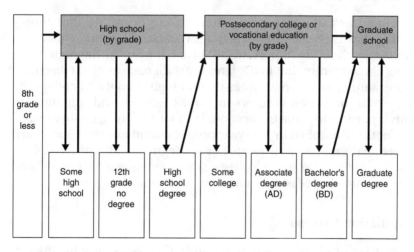

**Figure 3.2—Detailed Annual Flows to and from the Postelementary
Education System**

ber who leave school, and the number who continue on to the next grade. It also projects the annual number of people who return to school at various levels after having been out of school. Finally, and most important, the model projects the level of education achieved when people leave the educational system.

The counts of people in and out of school and the accounting of flows between the various in-school and out-of-school categories are all done by age of person. The population accounts keep track of ages 0 to 75+. People born outside the United States who later immigrate to the United States enter the model's accounts according to the year in which they arrive and their age and level of education upon arrival. The in-school accounts keep track of ages 13 to 40; age 13 recognizes the earliest entries into 9th grade. Including in-school ages up to 40 recognizes people obtaining degrees after having spent time out of school. The age dimension in the model is extremely important because flow rates vary considerably as people age. For example, older students are more likely than younger students to be part-time, a likelihood that is reflected in the annual school continuation rates and graduation rates. Moreover, keeping track of the age dimension enables us to predict the distribution of ages at which various population groups earn their degrees under alternative education policies.

Keeping track of which grade students are in (rather that simply noting that they are in high school, vocational school, college, or graduate school) is important because behavior in the early years differs greatly from that in the later years for each level of education. For example, the dropout rates in both high school and college are higher for juniors and seniors than for freshmen and sophomores. This is particularly true in vocational school and college, where many students are enrolled in two-year programs and exit the educational system with an associate degree or no degree at all. Our model explicitly notes whether a college student achieves a degree and whether that degree is an associate or a bachelor's degree.

Population Groups

Because educational attainment and fertility rates have historically varied among different groups in the population, the model tracks 20 population groups differentiated by the following characteristics:

Ethnicity	Nativity, or Immigration Status	Gender
Asian	Native-born	Male
Black	Immigrant	Female
Mexican		
Other Hispanic		
Non-Hispanic white		

Among Hispanics we distinguish between those of Mexican origin and "Other Hispanics" for two reasons: members of the first group are much less likely than members of the second group to attend or complete college; and Mexicans are the largest single group of Hispanics in the United States (Vernez and Abrahamse, 1996; Suarez-Orozco and Suarez-Orozco, 1995). And we distinguish between immigrants and native-borns within each social/ethnic group because of similarly significant differences between the two populations, reflecting in part the fact that the majority of foreign-born residents are educated primarily in their country of origin. For instance, Mexican native-borns are three times more likely to attend some college than are Mexican immigrants. European immigrants, in contrast, are more likely to have completed college than are European native-borns (Vernez and Abrahamse, 1996; McCarthy and Vernez, 1997; National Research Council, 1997). Immigrants also generally have higher fertility rates than do native-borns. For instance, in 1990, foreign-born married women age 40 to 44 had raised an average of 2.5 children, compared to 2.2 for native-born women of the same age. Women from Mexico, however, had raised nearly twice as many children (an average of 3.8) as most other immigrants and native-born women by that age (Vernez, 1999).

OPERATIONALIZING THE MODEL

To become operational, the RAND Education Simulation Model requires several inputs: (1) a set of in-school and out-of-school transition rates for each grade and each age, (2) birth and death rates, (3) international migration flows, and (4) in- and outmigration rates between California and the rest of the nation. These inputs are specific to each population group and age and can be changed at will. The benchmark model (referred to here as the base case) was calibrated using the data described next.

Education Flow Rates

The base case model was calibrated using the educational transition probabilities and educational attainment measured in the 1992, 1993, and 1994 Current Population Surveys (CPSs). The CPS asks whether a person is currently in school and whether he/she was in school last year. If the person is currently in school, CPS asks the grade; if the person is not in school, CPS asks the highest educational attainment. Answers to these questions provided the information we needed to estimate probabilities of transition from out-of-school into school, from one grade to another, and from school to out-of-school by ethnicity, gender, and age at the national level. In other words, this information enabled us to estimate the annual flow rates shown in Figure 3.2. However, the CPS sample contains too few observations to make state-specific estimates. To overcome this limitation, we used 1990 Census data on current educational attainment. We adjusted the CPS transition rates estimated at the national level, by population group, up and down as necessary to replicate the educational attainment observed for California and the rest of the nation in the 1990 Census. For instance, if the proportion of people completing high school for a given population group in California was higher than the national average, then the continuation rate during high school for that group in California was increased until the predicted proportion completing high school agreed with the observed proportion completing high school.

Also, the 1992 to 1994 CPSs did not contain information on immigration status.[2] In this case, we could not use the 1990 Census data to make adjustments, because we could not assume that the educational distribution of immigrants arriving before and after 1990 was equal. Hence, we assumed that the flow rates estimated for native-borns also applied to immigrants of the same ethnicity, gender, and place of origin. Recent studies (Vernez and Abrahamse, 1996;

---

[2]CPS started collecting information on immigration status in 1996. In the future, we expect to update the base case model periodically with the latest available information.

Suarez-Orozco and Suarez-Orozco, 1995) indicate that immigrants who come to the United States as children and enter the U.S. school system before 10th grade attain a level of education equal to or somewhat higher than that of native-borns of the same ethnicity and gender. For these foreign-born children, our assumption is not unduly biased. For immigrants who arrive as adults, however, it may overestimate their eventual educational attainment because it assumes, for instance, that a 20-year-old Mexican who arrives in the United States with fewer than 12 years of education has the same probability of going back to school as a native-born Mexican of the same age and level of education. Chapter Five assesses the sensitivity of our results to this assumption; Appendix E contains our estimates of flow rates in and out of education.

Demographic Inputs

For the base case, we used the birth and death rates that the U.S. Bureau of the Census used in making its "middle series" projection of the U.S. resident population to year 2050. For immigration, we used the 1990 Census immigration rates that prevailed during the 1985–1990 period, which averaged an aggregate 930,000 new legal and illegal immigrants annually. If anything, this latter flow is conservative; the annual number of immigrants in the 1990s has averaged in excess of 1 million.

Finally, we used the 1990 Census measured rates of in- and outmigration (by age, ethnicity, educational attainment, and gender) between California and the rest of the nation during the 1985–1990 period. The birth, death, and immigration rates used in our analyses are included in Appendix F.

Full-Time Equivalent Students

The model keeps track of individuals in and out of school or college in each of the above population groups regardless of whether they are enrolled full-time or part-time. To translate enrollment into required educational resources, we adjusted for the fact that not all students are full-time. Because the proportion of time that students attend school varies by population group and by student age, a ratio of full-time equivalent (FTE) students to enrollment (the "FTE ratio") was constructed separately for each population group and by age of student, again using the 1992–1994 CPS data. The FTE ratio at each grade was estimated as 1.0 minus the proportion of students remaining in the same grade for the next year.

Figure 3.3 illustrates the average estimates of FTE ratio by grade for the nation as a whole. The FTE ratio declines as the educational level increases. It is almost 100 percent for the high school grades, about 85 percent for the college grades, and about 75 percent for graduate school. This general pattern holds for the different population groups at different ages, but the specific numbers vary considerably.

Education Cost Assumptions

The costs of education fluctuate widely by state and within states by type of institutions and level of education. For this initial effort, we assumed that California's average costs would be reflective of national average costs (see discussion below). We used average operating cost estimates from public postelementary educational institu-

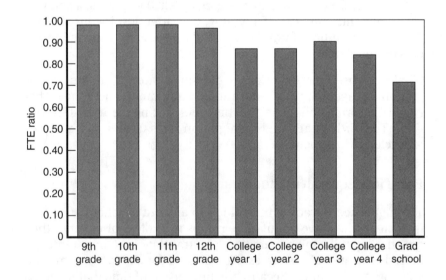

Figure 3.3—Ratio of Full-Time Equivalent Students to U.S. Enrollment,
1992

tions in California. Krop, Carroll, and Ross (1995) estimated the average annual cost per high school pupil in California to be $5,983 (1997 dollars); Shires (1996) estimated the average annual cost per FTE in California postsecondary institutions to be $3,248 in the community colleges; $9,911 in the California State Universities; and $20,269 at the University of California. The postsecondary education costs were weighted by FTE enrollment in each type of institution to produce estimates per level of education—i.e., lower-division college (freshmen and sophomores), upper-division college (juniors and seniors), and graduate school. This adjustment was required because our model traces students in and out of education by grade but not by type of institution.

Table 3.1 shows the resulting average annual operating cost estimates per level of education. To these estimates we added estimates of the annualized per-FTE capital costs to develop new physical capacity—i.e., estimates of the costs associated with expanding existing educational institutions to accommodate the projected increase in demand for education in California. Appendix G contains more details on our estimates of education costs.

In subsequent chapters, we show how we used these annualized average cost estimates per FTE to project the aggregate costs of changing demands in education. In interpreting our results, it is critical that the reader understand the limitations of our cost assumptions.

First, our estimates include total operating and capital expenditures regardless of who pays for them. At the high school level, nearly all costs are borne by the public. At the postsecondary level, the public

Table 3.1

Average Annual Cost per Full-Time Equivalent, 1997
(1997 dollars)

Annual Cost	High School	College		
		Lower Division	Upper Division	Graduate School
Operating cost	5,983	4,454	13,143	20,269
Capital cost	897	1,048	2,078	3,345
Total cost	6,880	5,502	15,221	23,614

SOURCES: Calculated from Krop, Carroll, and Ross, 1995; Shires, 1996; and Governor, State of California, *Governor's Budget Summary 1997–98.*

currently pays a national average of two-thirds of the total operating expenditures; students and other sources pay the other third in the form of tuition and fees. Considering that the minority students who are the focus of this study would most likely require outright public grants or low-interest publicly guaranteed loans to cover their share of tuition and fees, our use of total costs may reasonably reflect the public costs of increasing their educational attainment.

Second, as mentioned earlier, we assumed that the average costs per FTE in California reflect averages in the rest of the nation. For high school costs, this assumption is conservative, since California's average expenditures per pupil in K–12 are about 17 percent lower than the national average.[3] As for postsecondary education, California's average cost of public higher education is below the national average ($6,043 vs. $8,608) due to the state's extensive use of community colleges, whereas its cost of graduate education is above the national average. National estimates comparable to those we have for California on operating costs per type of higher education institution are not available. In the aggregate, however, the national average educational and general expenditures in public higher education per FTE are comparable to those in California: $11,841 vs. $11,463.[4]

Third, we chose to use average rather than marginal operating costs. Arguably, where there is excess capacity in the education system, marginal costs (i.e., the costs of providing education to one additional student) will always be lower than average costs because some expenses (e.g., facility maintenance, security, and even some staff) are fixed regardless of the number of students enrolled. In such a case, the differential between average and marginal costs can be as large as 50 percent, so our estimates of cost would be overestimated proportionately. However, if there is no excess capacity and new facilities and staff are thus needed to accommodate an increase in

---

[3]For instance, the *Digest of Education Statistics* (http://www.nces.ed.gov/pubs/digest97, Table 168) reports that current expenditures per pupil in 1994–1995 averaged $5,988 in the nation, compared to $4,992 in California. However, the reported current expenditures do not include all costs. The *Digest* indicates that the ratio of total to current expenditures in K–12 is about 1.12. Further adjusted by the CPI, the *Digest*'s California average cost per pupil equals $6,038, which is close to our own $5,983.

[4]Figures are for 1994–1995 and are computed from *Digest of Education Statistics*, Tables 347 and 201, at http://www.nces.ed.gov/pubs/digest97.

enrollment, the additional costs are more likely to be equal to, and may even exceed, the current average costs. The rapid growth of the school-age population in states where Hispanics are concentrated, including California, is already stretching the states' existing capacity to the limits and justifies our choice of using average rather than marginal operating costs in our estimates. We included average capital costs for new construction in our estimates for the same reason.

Finally, the reader should keep in mind that our estimates of costs—just as our estimates of benefits—are projections based on the assumption that current educational practices and policies will continue unaltered. They are not, however, predictions that these practices and policies will continue. Several changes in policies or practices may alter our estimates of costs. For instance, institutions may reduce some of their services, such as student support services, public service, and other services they currently provide to the community. Alternatively, all or most of the increase in enrollment in postsecondary education could be initially directed to community colleges and/or an expanded vocational education system. In these events, costs would be lower than our estimates, which are based on the distribution of additional enrollment across types of postsecondary institutions being similar to the current distribution. Alternatively, distance learning might negate the need for new facilities and decrease the current average costs of providing higher education. Indeed, the costs of education are themselves a variable that can be influenced by changes in education policies and/or practices.

OUTPUTS OF THE MODEL

The outputs generated by the RAND Education Simulation Model are listed below. They are for each of 76 years (0 to 75) in each of the population groups (20 for California and 20 for the rest of the nation). The model also generates summary tables that aggregate this detailed information so as to facilitate analysis.

- Number of people in each age cohort at a specified time.

- Educational attainment of each population group at a specified age.

- Student enrollment and full-time equivalent (FTE) student enrollment in each of four levels of education: high school, lower-
  division college, upper-division college, and graduate school.

- Costs of education at each of four levels of education: high
  school, lower-division college, upper-division college, and graduate school.

Using Chapter Two's estimates of government spending, tax revenues, and income per level of education, the model also provides
the following estimates for each population group and each age:

- Public spending for each of the following programs:
    - Welfare
    - Food stamps
    - SSI
    - Unemployment insurance
    - Medicaid
    - Medicare
    - Social Security
    - Lunch and breakfast programs
    - Energy assistance
    - Criminal justice
- Tax revenues by source:
    - Social insurance contributions (FICA)
    - Federal income tax
    - State taxes
- Posttransfer individual income

USES AND LIMITATIONS OF THE MODEL

The flexible structure of the RAND Education Simulation Model—it
is built as a collection of Excel spreadsheets—allows it to be used for
multiple purposes. It can be used to follow a cohort of people as they
age and obtain various amounts of education. This *cohort* version of
the model is particularly useful in explicitly assessing the effects of
changes in education, migration, or other policies that are intended
to directly (or that may indirectly) affect the education transition

rates of specific groups of the population or alter other inputs, such as internal and international migration rates and/or composition. In Chapter Five, we use this version of the model to assess the effects on enrollment, education costs, and government spending of closing the educational attainment gap between non-Hispanic whites and blacks and Hispanics. And in Chapter Six, we use this version of the model to assess the effects of immigration policies on the demand for education.

The model can also be used to project, year by year into the future, student enrollments, educational attainment and costs, and public spending under current trends or under alternative educational interventions. This *dynamic* version of the model is useful for assessing changes in demand placed on the various levels of the education system over time or in some future year. In Chapter Four, this version of the model is used to project the expected size of the population and its educational attainment at a specified future year while holding today's education transition rates, fertility rates, and immigration patterns constant.

In using and interpreting the outcomes from our model, the reader should keep in mind two important considerations. First, when assessing the outcomes of alternative scenarios, the focus should be on the relative differences in outcomes rather than on the estimated absolute outcomes of the scenarios. Since the assumptions we made in estimating costs and benefits are common to all alternatives considered, they do not have as much of an effect on the differences between alternatives.

A second consideration is that the model outcomes are projections based on holding a set of trends and/or policies constant. They are not a prediction of whether these trends or policies will or should be maintained. Indeed, the very purpose of doing the kind of analysis we performed is to develop the information and provide the guidance needed to assess whether it may be desirable to alter current public policies.

Chapter Four

EFFECTS OF DEMOGRAPHIC CHANGE ON EDUCATIONAL ATTAINMENT

What will the educational attainment of the population be if nothing is done to close the educational gap between non-Hispanic whites and blacks and Hispanics? This chapter explores this question by comparing the projected characteristics of the 2015 population age 25 or older to the characteristics of their 1990 counterparts. We first compare the size and ethnic composition of the actual 1990 and projected 2015 populations. We then compare the overall distribution of educational attainment between the two years. In the last section, we examine how the gap in educational attainment between ethnic groups is projected to change over time.

When interpreting the projections presented in this chapter, the reader should keep in mind that long-term projections of demographic and educational changes are based on many behavioral assumptions that, as past experience suggests, often prove to be wrong. Therefore, these projections should not be interpreted as a description of what the population is likely to look like in year 2015. Rather, they should be seen as a picture of what might be if current behavior and policies do not change. As detailed in Chapter Three, the fertility and death rates, internal and international migration patterns, and educational patterns used in our projections are those prevailing in the late 1980s, early 1990s. These rates and patterns are not static; they change constantly over time. As appropriate, we discuss how changes in these parameters might affect our projections.

PROJECTED SIZE AND COMPOSITION OF ADULT POPULATION

We project a 19 percent increase (from 157 million in 1990 to 187 million by year 2015) in the nation's adult population age 25 or older. This projection for the nation as a whole is seemingly conservative, being slightly above the low (184 million) projection by the U.S. Bureau of the Census. The Census's middle and high projections for the U.S. adult population by 2015 are 200 and 216 million, respectively. The main difference between the Census and our estimates stems from our more conservative assumption regarding immigration. We assume that current efforts to curb illegal immigration will be sustained and will eventually have some measure of success. We also assume that the 1970s and 1980s conflicts that fueled large flows of refugees to the United States from Southeast Asia and Central America will not recur, and hence that we can expect immigration from these regions to continue at levels comparable to current ones, rather than increasing.

We project that California's adult population will grow three times faster than the nation's; by 2015, it will be 55 percent larger than it was in 1990. Native-borns will make up only about one-third of the increase in the California population, and a majority of them will be children of the immigrants who have settled in the state since the 1970s. The bulk of the increase in population size will be due to immigration. We project that, overall, 39 percent of the 2015 California population will be foreign-born, compared to 25 percent of the 1990 population. In the rest of the nation, this pattern will be reversed. There, according to our projections, immigration will account for one-third of the increase in the population, and native-borns will account for the remaining two-thirds. The share of immigrants in the rest of the nation is projected to increase to 12 percent in 2015, up from 8 percent in the 1990 population. (See Figure 4.1.)

The ethnic composition of California and the rest of the nation is also projected to increasingly diverge. We project that minorities will account for more than half the population in California and that non-Hispanic whites will continue to account for the largest share of the population in the rest of the nation (Figure 4.2). In California, the share of the population of Mexican origin is projected to double (from 15 to 27 percent), as is the share of Asians (from 9 to 16 per-

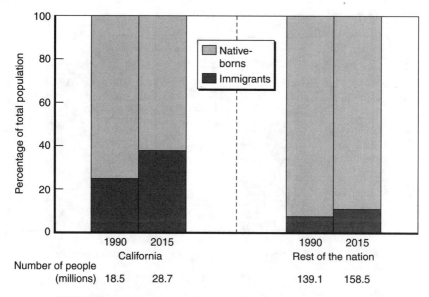

Number of people
(millions)   18.5   28.7   139.1   158.5

SOURCES: 1990 Public Use Samples (PUMs) of the U.S. Bureau of the
Census and RAND Education Simulation Model.

**Figure 4.1—Distribution of Adult Population by Nativity, California and
Rest of the Nation, 1990 and Projected for 2015**

cent). Both blacks and non-Hispanic whites are projected to see
their shares diminish. These compositional shifts reflect a projected
continuation of high immigration of Asians and Hispanics into California and a projected continuation of the higher fertility rates of
these ethnic groups.[1]

By contrast, non-Hispanic whites, and to a lesser extent blacks, are
projected to continue to dominate the 2015 adult population in the
rest of the nation. Non-Hispanic whites will maintain a 73 percent
share, compared to 82 percent in 1990. And, unlike in California,
blacks are projected to increase their share from 11 to 13 percent by
2015, and to continue to be more numerous than Hispanics. And
although we project that the shares of both Hispanics and Asians will

---

[1]For instance, compared to the fertility rate for native-born non-Hispanic white
women, that for immigrant Mexican women is 70 percent higher and that for native-
born Hispanic women is 30 percent higher (Vernez, 1999).

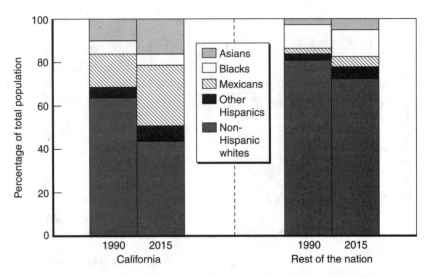

SOURCES: 1990 PUMs of the U.S. Bureau of the Census and RAND Education Simulation Model.

Figure 4.2—Ethnic Composition of Adult Population, California and Rest of the Nation, 1990 and Projected for 2015

increase in the rest of the nation, they will remain below 10 percent for the first group and below 5 percent for the second.

Based on our projections of these growing disparities in the ethnic composition of the population across states, we project that California will educate about 42 percent of all Hispanics in the nation and that more than half of its student body will eventually be blacks and Hispanics. By contrast, less than one-third of the student body in the rest of the nation is projected to be blacks and Hispanics, with both groups about equally numerous. California is also projected to eventually educate more than 40 percent of the Asian population in the nation.

When interpreting these trends, the reader should keep in mind that the projected ethnic groupings in year 2015 reflect the self-reported categorization used in 1990. This categorization may well no longer hold by 2015 and beyond. As the number and geographic concentration of Asians and Hispanics have increased, so has the frequency of intermarriage between ethnic groups, most particularly between

Hispanics and non-Hispanic whites, between Asians and non-Hispanic whites, and between Asians and Hispanics. How the children of these increasingly numerous mixed-ethnicity marriages are going to classify themselves is anyone's guess. And when and if they do classify themselves, what will be the meaning of the resulting categorization?

PROJECTED INCREASE IN EDUCATIONAL ATTAINMENT

Overall Population

We project that the overall educational attainment of the 2015 population age 25 or older will be higher than that of the 1990 population of the same age—in spite of the large increase in the share of minorities, continued immigration, and the continued low relative educational performance of blacks and Hispanics (Figure 4.3).

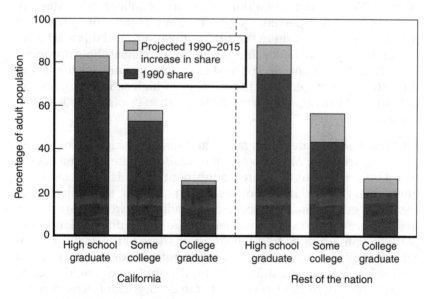

SOURCES: 1990 PUMs of the U.S. Bureau of the Census and RAND Education Simulation Model.

Figure 4.3—Educational Attainment of Adult Population, California and Rest of the Nation, 1990 and Projected for 2015

This is expected to be particularly the case in the rest of the nation, where the share of college graduates is projected to increase from 20 percent in 1990 to 26 percent in 2015. The share of the population with some college is also projected to increase, from 45 to 56 percent. This increase in the share of college-educated adults will be accompanied by a sizable decline in the share of high school dropouts, from 25 percent in 1990 to 12 percent in the 2015 cohort—a decline large enough to result in a near halving in the number of high school dropouts (from 34 to 19 million) from 1990 to 2015.

This upgrading in the educational attainment of the overall adult population reflects the dynamic demographic process—over a 25-year period—of older, less-educated people dying and being replaced by new, more-educated entrants into adulthood.[2]

The educational attainment of California's adult population is also projected to increase, but by less than is the case for the rest of the nation. We project that California's share of college graduates will increase by only 2 percentage points, from 23 percent in the 1990 population to 25 percent in the 2015 population. And this will be accompanied by a smaller decline in the share of high school dropouts, from 24 to 18 percent. In contrast to our projections for the rest of the nation, we project that the number of high school dropouts in California's 2015 population will be larger than it was in 1990—5 vs. 4 million.

The disproportionate immigration and relatively high share of Hispanics of primarily Mexican origin in California are why the educational attainment of the state's adult population is projected to be lower than that for the rest of the nation. Indeed, the projected increase in educational attainment in California would turn into a deficit were the growth in its share of the Hispanic population not partially compensated by a growth in its share of the Asian population. If California's Asian population is not considered, the share of college graduates in California's adult population would decline from 23 percent in 1990 to 19 percent in 2015, which is 6 percentage points lower than otherwise projected.

---

[2]Those being replaced were educated in the first half of the century, before the post–World War II expansion of educational opportunities, most particularly in higher education.

Ethnic Groups

Just as the education of the overall adult population is projected to increase, so is the educational attainment of each ethnic group. However, the increase is typically larger for each ethnic group than it is for the population as a whole, underlining the strength of the effect of the compositional change taking place in this country. Figure 4.4 illustrates this pattern for California. The pattern is similar in the rest of the nation (see Appendix H).

For the Mexican population, the increase in educational attainment between 1990 and 2015 is projected to be reflected mostly in increased shares of high school graduates and persons with some college. The Mexican share of college graduates is projected to increase

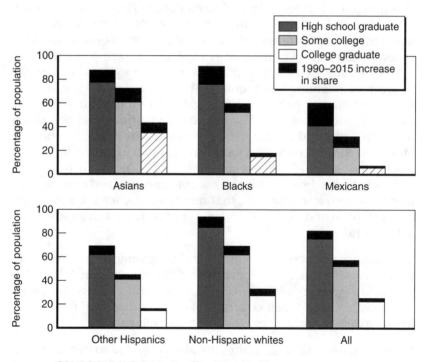

SOURCE: RAND Education Simulation Model.

Figure 4.4—Projected Increase in Educational Attainment of Adult Population by Ethnicity, California, 1990–2015

only slightly, from 5 to 7 percent in California and from 7 to 9 percent in the rest of the nation. The share of high school dropouts, however, is projected to decline from 50 to less than 40 percent.

For Asians, by contrast, the increase in educational attainment is projected to be the largest at the college level, including in the share of college graduates. In 1990, Asians were already more educated than any other ethnic group. We project not only that this pattern will be maintained in 2015, but that the gap between Asians and other ethnic groups will increase. For instance, in California, the gap in the share of college graduates between Asians and Mexicans in the 1990 cohort was 29 percentage points. This gap is projected to increase by nearly 7 percentage points, to 36 percentage points, by 2015.

The projected increases in the educational attainment of Asians, Mexicans, and Other Hispanics are the results of the intergenerational process of increasing educational attainment for subsequent generations of immigrants that is expected to take place between 1990 and 2015. Nowhere is this process more evident than in the Mexican population. The majority of immigrants from Mexico arrive with fewer than 12 years of schooling, because the majority of Mexico's population does not obtain more than a primary school education (McCarthy and Vernez, 1997). However, their children, born in Mexico or the United States, receive most or all of their schooling in the United States and hence are more likely than their parents to complete high school. Their rates of college-going and college completion remain low, however, so it remains to be seen whether subsequent, third and higher generations of Mexicans will go to college at higher rates.

This pattern of increased educational attainment for subsequent generations is similar for Asians, except that the share of Asian adult immigrants who arrive in the United States with a college education is already high. And their children not only emulate their parents but increase the share of Asians who complete college.

Blacks and non-Hispanic whites are also projected to increase their educational attainment between 1990 and 2015. For example, the share of adult blacks in California who are high school dropouts is projected to be significantly lowered, to about 10 percent, by 2015

(Figure 4.4). The share for non-Hispanic whites who are dropouts was already the lowest of any ethnic group in 1990 and is projected to remain so in 2015. Non-Hispanic whites are also projected to increase their share of college graduates relatively more than any other ethnic group, with the exception of Asians.

PROJECTED INCREASE IN EDUCATIONAL ATTAINMENT GAP

Even though the educational attainment of each ethnic group is projected to increase between 1990 and 2015, so too is the gap in educational attainment between ethnic groups. Table 4.1 compares the differences (gaps in percentage points) between the share of non-Hispanic whites and the share of minorities—Asians, blacks, Mexicans, and Other Hispanics—who are high school graduates, have some college, and are college graduates between 1990 and 2015 in California. It shows that the gap in the share of college graduates between blacks and Hispanics, on the one hand, and non-Hispanic whites, on the other, is projected to increase. At the same time, Asians are projected to double their share of college graduates relative to non-Hispanic whites. The net results of these projected

Table 4.1

Difference Between the Share of Non-Hispanic Whites and the Shares of Minorities Completing Different Levels of Education, California, 1990–2015 (percentage points)

Ethnic Group	High School Graduates		Some College		College Graduates	
	1990	2015	1990	2015	1990	2015
Asians	8.3	5.9	1.6	−2.0	−6.7	−11.0
Blacks	9.9	3.3	10.2	10.2	13.1	14.9
Mexicans	44.1	33.9	39.0	38.7	20.9	25.2
Other Hispanics	22.8	24.2	20.9	25.2	12.3	16.7

SOURCES: 1990 PUMs of the U.S. Bureau of the Census and RAND Education Simulation Model.

NOTE: The ethnic group of reference is non-Hispanic white. The higher the positive numbers, the larger the gap in educational attainment for the ethnic group shown. The negative numbers shown for Asians indicate a gap favoring Asians compared to non-Hispanic whites, a gap that is projected to grow over time.

trends is that Asians and non-Hispanic whites will contribute the overwhelming majority (89 percent) of college graduates in year 2015 in California, potentially leading to an increase in economic disparities between these two ethnic groups, on the one hand, and Hispanics and blacks, on the other.

At the lower end of the educational distribution, the gap in the share of high school graduates between non-Hispanic whites and minorities is projected to decrease, more so for blacks than for Hispanics. Even so, the share of all high school dropouts who are Hispanics or blacks is projected to increase from 55 percent in 1990 to 73 percent in 2015.

The same pattern is projected for the rest of the nation, although it will be somewhat less pronounced.

CONCLUSIONS

The overall educational attainment of the adult population age 25 or older will, according to our projections, increase between 1990 and 2015 in spite of projected increased immigration and accelerated shifts in the ethnic composition of the population. This pattern of increased educational attainment is projected to take place across all ethnic groups, including Mexicans, Other Hispanics, and Asians. This reflects the dynamic process of older, less-educated people dying and being replaced by new, more-educated entrants into adulthood. It also reflects educational mobility across generations of immigrants.

However, the educational gap between blacks and Hispanics, on the one hand, and Asians and non-Hispanic whites, on the other, is projected to increase, most particularly in California. In that state, projections are that the first group will constitute an overwhelming majority (75 percent) of the state's high school dropouts and that the second group will constitute an overwhelming majority (89 percent) of the state's college graduates. Although less pronounced, our projected trends for the rest of the nation are similar.

Chapter Five

COSTS AND BENEFITS OF CLOSING THE EDUCATIONAL ATTAINMENT GAP FOR BLACKS AND HISPANICS

This chapter addresses the question: What would the benefits be and what would the costs be if blacks and Hispanics graduated from high school, went to college, and/or graduated from college at the same rate as non-Hispanic whites?[1]

- By how much would the educational attainment gap between non-Hispanic whites and blacks and Hispanics decrease?

- By how much would the overall educational attainment of the labor force increase?

- By how much would the secondary and postsecondary education capacity have to expand to accommodate the resulting increase in demand?

- What would the additional educational costs be?

- What public savings would the additional education generate, both by decreasing the demand for income transfer and social programs and by increasing tax revenues?

We considered four alternative goals that might be pursued as a way to increase the educational attainment of minorities. They are intro-

---

[1]We use non-Hispanic whites as the comparison group because they currently constitute the largest ethnic group. Asians, as a group, already outperform non-Hispanic whites in educational attainment, and we expect them to continue to do so.

duced first below. Then, the costs and benefits of meeting these goals are discussed, including the implications for closing the gap in educational attainment, the educational attainment of the labor force, the supply and costs of education, and public expenditures for social programs.

ALTERNATIVE GOALS

The nation's schools, colleges, and universities have implemented a large array of programs designed to increase the educational attainment of minorities. These programs range from high school dropout prevention programs to college outreach, remedial, and retention programs. All of these intervene at different points in the educational cycle. Some focus on high school students, some focus on facilitating the transition from high school to college, and some focus on minority students who are already enrolled in college. Without prejudging the relative effectiveness of these various intervention strategies, individually or in combination, we selected four alternative goals for closing the education gap:

Goal 1: Equalize High School Graduation Rates. This "high school" equalization goal considers that blacks and Hispanics remain in school and eventually graduate from high school at the same rate and at the same time as native-born non-Hispanic whites. The college-going, retention, and graduation rates of these three ethnic groups continue to differ as they have historically.

Goal 2: Equalize High School Graduation and First-Year College-Going Rates. This "college-going" equalization goal considers that blacks and Hispanics remain in primary and secondary school, graduate from high school, and then enroll in college at the same rate as native-born non-Hispanic whites. The college retention and graduation rates of these three groups continue to differ as they have historically.

Goal 3: Equalize College Retention Rates. This "college retention" equalization goal considers that blacks and Hispanics who currently enroll in the nation's colleges and universities go on to their sophomore, junior, and senior years and eventually graduate with a bachelor's degree at the same rate as native-born non-Hispanic whites.

The high school graduation and first year college enrollment rates of these three groups continue to differ as they have historically.

Goal 4: Equalize All Transition Rates In and Out of School. This "full equalization" goal considers that blacks and Hispanics remain in school, graduate from high school, go to and remain in college, and graduate from college at the same rate as native-born non-Hispanic whites. In other words, ethnic differences in the transition rates in and out of U.S. schools, colleges, and universities are equalized across all ethnic native-born groups. Note that because of expected continued immigration, this (as well as the other alternatives) does not mean equal outcomes. This is because most immigrants enter the country as adults and hence acquire additional education in the United States only at the rate at which native-born non-Hispanic white adults similarly educated and of the same age acquire additional education.[2]

We used the RAND Education Simulation Model (discussed in Chapter Three) to estimate the implications of our four alternative goals for the educational attainment gap, the educational attainment of the adult labor force in general, the supply and costs of education, and the public benefits generated by the additional education. We assessed these effects for both the state of California and the rest of the nation.

To facilitate interpretation of the results, we compare the implications of the four alternative goals for the cohort of children born in 1990. Following a cohort over its life cycle is the proper way to do cost-effectiveness analysis of interventions in the education system. The results are unencumbered by data for cohorts that have already completed their schooling prior to the changes, as would be the case in cross-section analysis at one point in time, say, 2015. Also, the costs and benefits for a cohort of people can be completely accounted for, and the timing of these costs and benefits is known, so the appropriate discounting of the future can be considered.

---

[2]We assessed the difference in the sensitivity of outcomes to this assumption vs. the less optimistic assumption that immigrants entering the country after the age of 16 do not acquire additional education in the United States. This is discussed throughout this chapter.

While our analysis focuses on the 1990 birth cohort, it is not static. Every year, as the cohort ages and moves through the U.S. education system, it is atritted by the death of some of its members and joined by immigrants of the same age who enter the U.S. education system (and hence our analysis). In addition, in the California analysis, some members of the cohort born in California move out of state while new members, born in the rest of the nation, move in.

Our comparisons of educational attainment are made for the 1990 cohort when it has reached age 40, in 2030, because existing data suggest that most members of the cohort will have completed their education by that age.[3] The outcomes of reaching each alternative goal are compared to the outcomes the cohort would have achieved had the gap in educational transitional rates between the different ethnic, nativity, and gender groups remained equal to that actually measured circa 1990, as described in Chapter Four.

This cohort outcome can also be interpreted as the educational attainment of the population in steady state. This interpretation is possible because, in steady state, the cross section at a point in time is just the sum of all ages in a cohort.

EFFECTS ON EDUCATIONAL ATTAINMENT GAP

Reduced Gap Between Ethnic Groups

We first examined the effects that meeting each of the alternative goals would have on the educational attainment gap between ethnic groups. We found that meeting any one of the goals would significantly close the gap in the share of high school graduates and college-educated between blacks and Hispanics and non-Hispanic whites, although in different proportions (see Figure 5.1).

Clearly the "full equalization" goal would increase minority educational attainment the most and would also close the gap relative to non-Hispanic whites the most. Low-educated Mexicans would gain the most. Under this plan, for Mexican 40-year-olds, the share who

---

[3]Savings to government and increased incomes, however, are computed over the lifetime of the cohort. Because they are discounted, savings beyond age 40 add little to present value of costs and benefits.

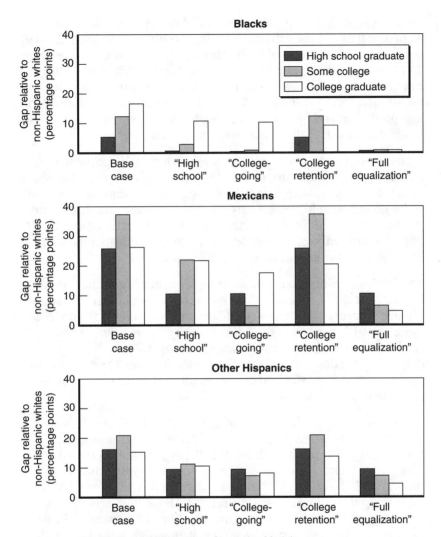

SOURCE: RAND Education Simulation Model.

NOTE: The shorter the bar, the lower the gap (difference) in educational attainment relative to non-Hispanic whites. The base case assumes current school-going rates will continue.

Figure 5.1—Projected Gap in Educational Attainment for Blacks and Hispanics Relative to Non-Hispanic Whites Under Alternative Goals, California, Cohort Age 40 in 2030

are college graduates in California would nearly quadruple (from 8 to 29 percent), the share with some college would double (from 37 to 67 percent), and the share of high school graduates would increase by 20 percent (from 70 to 85 percent). Still, even this plan would not fully close the gap relative to non-Hispanic whites. The Mexican population would still lag by 5 percentage points in its share of college graduates and by 10 percentage points in its share of high school graduates, as would the Other Hispanic population.

By contrast, blacks would reach parity with non-Hispanic whites at all levels of education under the "full equalization" goal. The share of blacks who are college graduates would double, and the share with some college would increase by 20 percent. Since the high school graduation rate of blacks in California already nearly equals that of non-Hispanic whites, there is only a nominal increase in the share of black high school graduates under this plan.

The "college-going" goal, which would equalize high school graduation rates and enrollment in the first year of college, offers the second highest improvement in the educational attainment of minorities. For blacks, it closes all of the education gap in the share of both high school graduates and some college (as the "full equalization" plan does). For Mexicans and Other Hispanics, it closes about half of this gap. The gap in the share of college graduates, however, is not cut as dramatically: by one-third for both blacks and Mexicans.

A comparison of the outcomes of the "high school" and "college retention" equalization goals for the three ethnic groups considered shows that the gap in the share of college graduates between Mexicans and blacks, on one hand, and non-Hispanic whites, on the other, would be similarly reduced either by focusing exclusively on increasing the college retention rates of those who are already enrolled in college ("college retention" goal) or by focusing exclusively, as is mostly the case currently, on equalizing high school graduation rates ("high school" goal). The gap in the share of college graduates among Mexicans would decrease by about 20 percent under both options, and that for blacks would decrease by about one-third.

Other Hispanics are the exception here. The gap in their share of college graduates would decrease significantly more if the focus were on increasing their high school graduation rate rather than increasing their college retention rate. The reason behind this outcome is that the college continuation and graduation rates of Other Hispanics already exceed those of both Mexicans and blacks and are closer than those of Mexicans and blacks to the rates experienced by non-Hispanic whites.

Increased Gap Between Natives and Immigrants

Immigration is the reason why the gap in educational attainment between Mexican and Other Hispanics and non-Hispanic whites is not fully closed, even under the "full equalization" goal. Our analysis assumed that immigrants would continue to arrive at the same rate and with the same educational levels as immigrants did in the latter part of the 1980s.[4] As is well documented (e.g., McCarthy and Vernez, 1997), the educational attainment of Mexican immigrants arriving in the United States is significantly lower than that of native-born Mexicans. And even though we assumed that immigrants who arrive in the United States as adults acquire additional education in the United States at the same rates as native-born adults of the same age and education,[5] the gap in educational attainment between immigrants and native-borns not only remains large but increases for our four alternative goals (Table 5.1). Whereas the share of Mexican immigrants who are college graduates is 3 percentage points lower than the share of native-born Mexican college graduates (6.1 vs. 8.9 percent) for the base case, this gap increases to 7 percentage points for the "high school" goal and 23 percentage points for the "full equalization" goal.

Our assumption that adult immigrants and adult native-borns of the same age and level of education acquire additional education in the United States at the same rate may be too optimistic, however. By and large, adult immigrants (especially low-educated immigrants) have an extremely low propensity for acquiring additional education

---

[4]We consider the effects of changes in immigration policies in the next chapter.

[5]This means, for instance, that a 20-year-old Mexican immigrant who has ten years of education upon arriving in the United States is assumed to go back to school at the same rate as a 20-year-old native-born Mexican who has only ten years of schooling.

Table 5.1

Projected Shares of Native-Born and Immigrant Mexican Men Born in
1990 That Would Be High School and College Graduates at Age 40
Under Alternative Educational Goals, California, 2030
(percent)

	Share of High School Graduates		Share of College Graduates	
	Native-Born	Immigrant	Native-Born	Immigrant
Base case	82.8	54.0	8.9	6.1
Goals				
"High school"	99.1	69.6	15.2	8.1
"College-going"	99.1	69.6	20.4	10.0
"College retention"	82.8	54.0	18.2	10.4
"Full equalization"	99.1	69.6	41.7	18.4

SOURCE: RAND Education Simulation Model.

after arriving in this country (Vernez, 1999).[6] Indeed, if we assumed
that adult immigrants did not acquire additional education, the resulting increase in the gap between native-borns and immigrants for
the alternative goals would be even larger. The gap in the share of
high school graduates between Mexican immigrants and native-
borns under the "full equalization" plan would increase from 30 to 42
percentage points, and the gap in the share of college graduates
would increase from 23 to 32 percentage points. These outcomes
underscore the importance of providing equal educational access to
immigrants and of encouraging them to avail themselves of educational opportunities.

Increased Gap Between Regions

The pattern of change in the educational attainment of minorities
relative to non-Hispanic whites that was observed for the four goals
for California is the same for the rest of the nation. However, in every
instance, the educational attainment of minorities is lower (Figure

---

[6]As noted earlier, this is not generally the case for immigrant children who arrive in
the United States before they reach age 15 or 16. These children attain an education
equal to or even higher than that of their native-born counterparts (Vernez and
Abrahamse, 1996).

5.2). For example, under the "full equalization" goal, the share of Mexican college graduates in the rest of the nation would be 25 percent, whereas it would be 29 percent in California. The same pattern is observable for blacks and Other Hispanics. Similarly, for the "college retention" goal, the share of black college graduates is projected to be 5 percentage points lower in the rest of the nation than in California (20 vs. 25 percent).

This differential in educational attainment between California and the rest of the nation reflects the fact that California has, on the average, a more developed postsecondary system than does the rest of

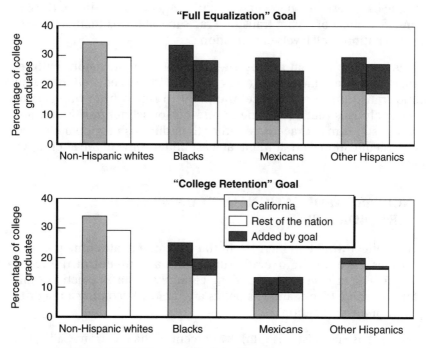

SOURCE: RAND Education Simulation Model.

NOTE: Each bar represents the share of each ethnic group projected to be college graduates. The dark portion of each bar indicates the increase in the share of college graduates above the base case.

Figure 5.2—Projected Educational Attainment in California and Rest of the Nation for 1990 Cohort Under Two of the Alternative Goals

the nation. The result is that non-Hispanic white (and other) residents of California attain, again on the average, a higher level of education. For instance, the share of high school graduates that continue on to postsecondary education is 15 percentage points higher in California than in the rest of the nation (72 vs. 57 percent).

Typically, the education gap between California and the rest of the nation for a specific minority group increases rather than decreases under the various goals considered. For instance, under the "full equalization" plan, the differential in the share of black college graduates between California and the rest of the nation increases from 3 to 5 percentage points. For Mexicans, this gap increases from none in the base case to 4 percentage points. Again, this is due to the cumulative effect of higher transition rates in California than in the rest of the nation at all levels of education.

This is not to say that the rest of the nation is homogenous with respect to education. Indeed, every state has its own education system and transition rates. Hence, the point to retain from this part of the analysis is that equalizing in-and-out-of-school transition rates across states may exacerbate rather than diminish regional disparities in educational attainment, at least under some of the alternative goals.

INCREASED EDUCATIONAL ATTAINMENT OF THE LABOR FORCE

What effect would an increase in the educational attainment of minorities have on the overall educational attainment of the labor force? The answer is, a great deal, certainly in states (such as California) where blacks and Hispanics are rapidly becoming a majority share of the population.

For the base case (status quo), 84 percent of the cohort in California is projected to graduate from high school, 59 percent to have some college, and 25 percent to graduate from college. With the exception of the "college retention" goal, all goals would increase the shares of the cohort who are high school graduates, have some college, and are college graduates (Figure 5.3). These shares would increase the least under the "high school" goal—by 6, 7, and 2 percentage points, respectively—and the most under the "full equalization" goal—the

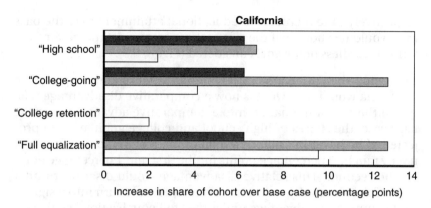

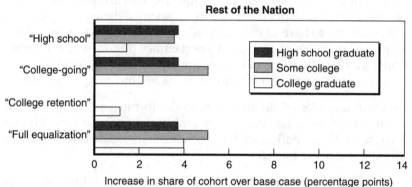

SOURCE: RAND Education Simulation Model.

NOTE: The bars represent the difference in shares (percentage points) between each goal and the base case for the cohort attaining the indicated level of education.

Figure 5.3—Projected Changes in the Educational Attainment at Age 40 of the Cohort Born in 1990 Under Alternative Goals, California and Rest of the Nation

share of college graduates alone would increase by 9 percentage points, going from 25 to 34 percent. The "high school" and "college retention" goals would generate equal, but lower, increases in the share of college graduates, from 25 to 27 percent.

In the rest of the nation, where the 1990 cohort is 15 percent black and 13 percent Hispanic (compared to California's 5 and 45 percent, respectively), the increases in educational attainment over the base case would be about half the size of the increases estimated for California regardless of the goal considered (Figure 5.3).

Increasing the educational attainment of blacks and Hispanics in California would turn what is now a comparative disadvantage relative to the rest of the nation into a comparative advantage. For the base case, the shares of high school and college graduates are projected to be lower in California than in the rest of the nation, albeit not by much: 3 percentage points for the first and 1 percentage point for the second. This relative disadvantage would disappear under each of the alternative goals, however, and would turn into a significant comparative advantage under the "full equalization" goal. Under this goal, California would go from having a deficit of 1 percentage point in its share of college graduates relative to the rest of the nation to having an advantage of 5 percentage points—i.e., California would increase its share of college graduates from 25 to 34 percent, compared to the rest of the nation's increase from 26 to 30 percent.

Similar though less dramatic shifts to California's advantage would occur under the other three, less ambitious goals, except for the "high school" alternative, under which the state would only reach par with the rest of the nation.

Note that the advantage gained by increasing the educational attainment of California's black and Hispanic minorities would take place in spite of our assumption that a disproportionately high proportion of low-educated immigrants will continue to settle in that state.

EFFECTS ON EDUCATIONAL INSTITUTIONS: INCREASED ENROLLMENTS AND COSTS

To achieve an increase in the educational attainment of blacks and Hispanics will necessitate an increase in the supply and hence the costs of educational services throughout the nation. Indeed, increasing the supply of these services is a necessary, although not sufficient, prerequisite.

How much more education would have to be supplied? Figure 5.4 displays the projected percent increase over the base case in FTE en-

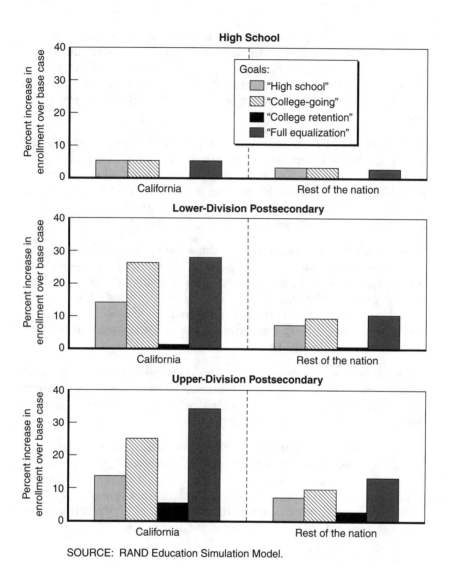

SOURCE: RAND Education Simulation Model.

Figure 5.4—Percent Increase in FTE Enrollment Under Alternative Goals, California and Rest of the Nation, by Level of Education

rollment for each of three levels of education—high school, lower-division postsecondary, and upper-division postsecondary—and each of our four goals. Regardless of which goal is considered, the increase in high school FTE students would be relatively small in both California and the rest of the nation: about 6 and 3 percent, respectively.[7]

The increase in FTE enrollment would be significantly larger in the postsecondary education system than in high school under the goals considered. For instance, in California, under the "full equalization" goal, FTE enrollment would increase by 28 percent in lower-division colleges (including two-year community colleges) and by more than one-third in upper-division postsecondary institutions.

The ripple effect across the entire education system of simply equalizing high school graduation rates—the "high school" goal—between non-Hispanic whites and the black and Hispanic minorities would also be sizable. Whereas FTE enrollment in California's high schools would increase by 6 percent, FTE enrollment in its lower- and upper-division postsecondary institutions would increase by more than twice as much—about 14 percent.

Of the goals considered, meeting the "college retention" alternative would impact education institutions the least. FTE postsecondary enrollment would increase a mere 1 percent in the lower division and 5 percent in the upper division.

Because the share of Hispanics and blacks in the rest of the nation is lower than the share in California (28 vs. 50 percent), the increase in FTE enrollment in the rest of the nation's educational institutions would be about half that projected for California (Figure 5.4). This difference underlines the highly differentiated effects resulting from the high concentration of minorities in California.

---

[7]The estimates of increases in FTE enrollment (and costs) were obtained by summing the estimated enrollment over the successive ages of the cohort (from 12 to 39) where participation in postelementary education occurs. Hence, these estimates can be interpreted as the required supply of educational services in steady state. Also, note that the increases in supply discussed here would be in addition to the increase in the supply of education expected to be needed simply to meet the increase in size of the student population due to population growth, as was documented in Chapter One. There, we stated our projection that the school-age population (age 0–24) will increase by 15 percent in the nation as a whole.

As FTE enrollment is projected to increase, so are the costs of education (Figure 5.5). Overall, meeting the "full equalization" goal would add to the costs of education about 21 percent in California and about 8 percent in the rest of the nation. This translates roughly to additional funding for education of (in 1997 dollars) about $9 billion annually in California and about $14 billion annually in the rest of the nation. These estimated costs are full costs at the steady state, i.e., when all successive cohorts of black and Hispanic students would attain levels of education similar to those of non-Hispanic whites. In practice, however, any programs that would meet these goals would be implemented over time, cohort by cohort, so that both the increments in enrollments and in costs would be absorbed not all at once, but over a period of years.

The costs of meeting the other three goals would be clearly lower than the costs of meeting the "full equalization" goal, with "college retention" being the cheapest. This latter goal would add 3 percent to the costs of education in California and half that amount in the rest of the nation. In exchange for this relatively small increment in costs, the share of college graduates among Mexicans in California

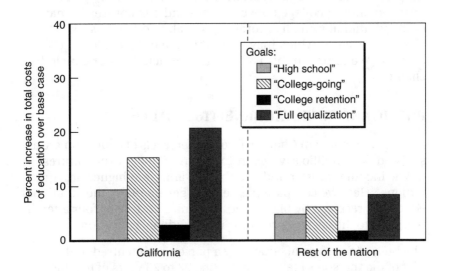

Figure 5.5—Percent Increase in Costs of Education Under Alternative Goals, California and Rest of the Nation

would double and that of blacks and Other Hispanics would increase by 40 and 9 percent, respectively.

Our estimates of costs to close the educational gap for blacks and Hispanics are based on current average costs per FTE student at each level of education (see Chapter Three for details and for a discussion of limitations). However, as we highlighted in Chapter Three, these estimated increases in costs are indicative and could be significantly altered by two factors—one that would lower and one that would increase them. First, where there is excess capacity in the education system, the marginal cost of accommodating the increased FTE enrollment is likely to be lower than the average cost. This may well be the case for those goals that result in a relatively small increment in FTE enrollment, such as the "college retention" goal. But for the goals that would result in a large increase in FTE enrollment—say, in excess of 10 percent—capacity may need to be expanded through new capital investments. In this case, the use of average costs may be most appropriate.

A second factor that may significantly alter our cost estimates concerns the potential need to provide additional educational and other support services to minority students. To successfully help them stay in school and in college above and beyond current trends may require additional remedial, tutoring, social, and family support services whose costs, which may be sizable, are not included in our estimates. We return to this issue in greater detail in our concluding chapter.

PUBLIC AND SOCIETAL BENEFITS AND COSTS

As we documented in Chapter Two, higher levels of education are associated with public savings in the form of lower expenditures for public income transfer and health programs, and higher tax contributions. Here we compare the benefits generated by the additional education received by blacks and Hispanics under our four alternative goals to the costs of providing the additional education.

The bulk of the costs of educating a person are incurred in the early part of that person's life (i.e., in the first 22 to 25 years of her/his life), whereas the benefits of that education are accrued mainly after the person leaves school or college and then over the remainder of her/his life. To overcome this differential in the timing of costs and benefits, we translated each cost and benefit into present value terms using a 4 percent discount rate. Our choice of this discount rate was somewhat arbitrary, for there is no consensus on what is an appropriate social discount rate (Baumol, 1979; Cummings, 1990). Estimates range from 2 to 10 percent in real, inflation-adjusted terms. Below, we also discuss the sensitivity of the estimated benefit/cost ratio to changes in the value of the discount rate.

Table 5.2 shows the benefit/cost ratios of increasing the education of blacks and Hispanics under our four goals. For each goal, two ratios are shown; they differ by what they include on the benefits side. The "public" ratio includes two benefits: the savings in public expenditures and the increase in tax revenues. The "societal" ratio includes these two public benefits plus the increase in individual (private) disposable income.

The estimated "public" benefits of increasing the education of blacks and Hispanics exceed the estimated costs of providing this education, regardless of the goal considered, in both California and the rest of the nation. For instance, the public benefit/cost ratio of 1.9 for the "full equalization" goal implies that every \$1 spent on education would save, over the long term, about \$1.90 in 1997 dollars in California. The public benefit/cost ratio is even more favorable in the rest of the nation, where every \$1 spent on the full plan would save

Table 5.2

Benefit/Cost Ratios of Reaching Alternative Education Goals for Blacks and Hispanics, California and Rest of the Nation

Goals	California		Rest of Nation	
	Public	Societal	Public	Societal
"High school"	2.4	4.6	3.3	5.7
"College-going"	2.1	4.3	3.0	5.4
"College retention"	1.4	3.3	1.2	2.7
"Full equalization"	1.9	4.1	2.6	4.9

SOURCE: Appendix I, Table I.1.

NOTE: See text discussion of Table 5.2 for definition of "public" and "societal" benefit/cost ratios. A 4 percent discount rate was used to estimate these ratios.

$2.60 in 1997 dollars. Typically, the benefit/cost ratio is larger in the rest of the nation than it is in California.

The public benefit/cost ratio for closing the educational attainment gap also varies according to the goal considered. The "high school" goal is the most cost-effective of the alternatives for both California and the rest of the nation. Its ratio of public benefits to costs is 2.4 in California and 3.3 in the rest of the nation. As Chapter Two discusses, this is because the savings in the use of government programs are the largest when an individual's education increases from high school dropout to high school graduate, and they are the smallest when an individual's education increases from having some college to college graduate.

The "college retention" goal is the least cost-effective. Its benefit/ cost ratio is 1.4 in California and 1.2 in the rest of the nation.

Savings in government expenditures on income transfers and other social programs account for one-third to one-half of the public benefits associated with closing the educational attainment gap for minorities. Increases in tax revenues and in contributions to Social Security and Medicare account for the rest of the public savings.[8]

Increases in educational attainment not only result in public benefits, they also are associated with increases in personal (or private) income for the individual whose education has been increased (see Chapter Two). When these private benefits (in the form of added net disposable income) are added to the "public" benefits, the result is the "societal" benefits. As Table 5.2 shows, the societal benefit/cost ratio associated with each goal is nearly double the public benefit/cost ratio. For instance, every $1 invested to meet the "full equalization" goal in California would lead to $4.10 in combined governmental savings and increased disposable income. This societal benefit/cost ratio is 4.9 in the rest of the nation.

As we indicated earlier, the public and societal benefit/cost ratios for closing the educational attainment gap for Hispanics and blacks are sensitive to the choice of discount rate. Choosing a high discount

---

[8]Figure I.1 in Appendix I shows the distribution of public savings by source under the "full equalization" goal.

rate—e.g., 10 percent—implies that, as a society, we value the present much more than the future. In other words, it implies that we are more concerned about our present economic well-being than about our well-being ten or 20 years down the road, and that we certainly are not very concerned about the well-being of the next generation. In contrast, choosing a low discount rate implies that we care not only about our economic well-being ten, 20, or more years down the road, but also in some measure about the well-being of both our children and the children of our neighbors.

With this in mind, two questions arise. The first is, How high must the discount rate be for the present value of the costs of closing the educational attainment gap to exceed the benefits? The answer (contained in Table 5.3) is that the discount rate must exceed 10 percent—i.e., must be higher than the highest discount rate suggested by economists as a reasonable societal discount rate for public investments. Even to meet the "college retention" goal, which has the lowest "societal" benefit/cost ratio of the four options considered, this ratio remains greater than 1 if the discount rate is as high as 10

Table 5.3

Benefit/Cost Ratios for Increasing the Education of Blacks and Hispanics Under Alternative Goals and Discount Rates, California and Rest of the Nation

	Discount Rate					
	6 Percent		8 Percent		10 Percent	
Goals	Public	Societal	Public	Societal	Public	Societal
	California					
"High school"	1.8	3.3	1.4	2.6	1.1	2.0
"College-going"	1.6	3.2	1.3	2.5	1.1	2.0
"College retention"	0.0	2.4	0.8	1.8	0.6	1.5
"Full equalization"	1.5	3.0	1.2	2.4	1.0	1.9
	Rest of the Nation					
"High school"	2.5	4.3	2.0	3.3	1.7	2.7
"College-going"	2.3	4.1	1.9	3.2	1.6	2.6
"College retention"	0.9	2.0	0.7	1.6	0.6	1.2
"Full equalization"	2.0	3.7	1.6	2.9	1.4	2.4

SOURCE: RAND Education Simulation Model.

percent: 1.2 in the rest of the nation and 1.5 in California. However, if only public savings are considered, the "public" benefit/cost ratio for this goal becomes less than 1 as the discount rate used equals 8 percent or more. For the other three goals, the discount rate must equal or exceed 10 percent for the "public" benefit/cost ratio to equal or fall below 1.

The second question that arises is, How many years will it take for the public sector, and society more generally, to recoup the increased investments made in the education of blacks and Hispanics? In other words, how many years will it take until the benefits derived from the increased level of education begin to exceed the costs of providing that increased education? The answer to this question varies depending on the goal considered.

For the "full equalization" goal, and for California, total societal benefits exceed costs by age 25, for an average payback period of about 6 years.[9] If we consider only public savings to the government, benefits would exceed costs by age 32, for an average payback period of 13 years. Figure 5.6 shows the cumulative distribution of the present value of benefits and costs as the cohort ages under the "full equalization" goal. It shows that the added costs (over the base case) begin at age 14, as the cohort enters middle school,[10] and continue until age 40, when most adults have completed their education. The bulk of the additional expenditures, however, occur between the ages of 16 (when dropping out becomes more frequent) and 22 (when students begin to complete college). The public and societal benefits, by contrast, begin to accumulate at age 18 (because this is the age at which the increase in education is first acquired under our four alternatives) and continue to accumulate throughout the life of the individual. In Figure 5.6, the present value of the benefits is divided by the present value of the costs, so the two benefit lines represent costs/effectiveness ratios. Of particular interest are the points at which the benefit lines cross the cost line. At that point, and that age of the cohort, the present value of benefits equals costs. It shows that

---

[9]Since increases in education costs start at about age 16 and the bulk of them are completed by age 22, the average increased expenditure is at 19, making the payback period 25 – 19, or 6, years.

[10]Until then, there is no real difference in school enrollment between ethnic groups.

the payback time period relative to government savings even under the "full equalization" alternative would be lower in the rest of the nation than in California—8 vs. 13 years.

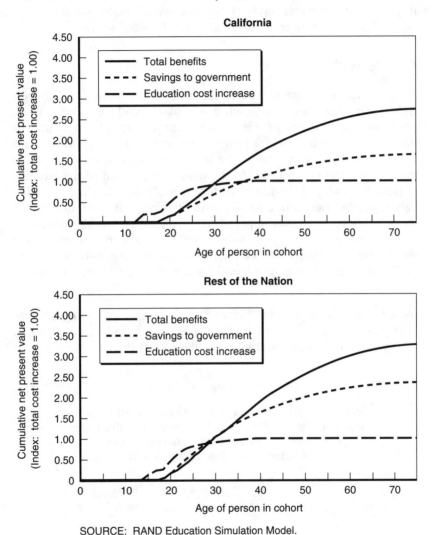

SOURCE: RAND Education Simulation Model.

Figure 5.6—Net Present Value of Cumulative Cost and Benefits over Life of Cohort: "Full Equalization" Alternative, California and Rest of the Nation

The payback times vary depending on the goal considered. Table 5.4 compares the average number of years it would take for public benefits and societal benefits to exceed costs under each of the four alternatives. The shortest payback periods would occur for the "high school" goal, the longest for the "college retention" goal.

CONCLUSIONS

An investment in closing the educational attainment gap between non-Hispanic whites, on one hand, and blacks and Hispanics, on the other, would clearly pay for itself in the form of long-term savings in income transfer and social programs, increased tax revenues, and increased disposable income for the individuals involved. This is particularly the case in California, where nearly half of the student population today is Hispanic. In that state, failure to close the education gap for these students will result in a large share of future (and larger) cohorts being unprepared to compete in a labor market that increasingly requires at least some postsecondary education. It also would lead to an increase in educational inequalities between blacks and Hispanics, on one hand, and Asians and non-Hispanic whites, on the other.

Increasing the education of blacks and Hispanics would require sizable increases in the capacity of mainly postsecondary educational institutions and hence significant dollar investments. One obstacle

Table 5.4

Average Number of Years Needed to Equalize the Present
Value of Costs and Benefits of Increasing the Education of
Blacks and Hispanics Under Alternative Goals,
California and Rest of the Nation

Goals	California		Rest of the Nation	
	Public	Societal	Public	Societal
"High school"	8	4	5	4
"College-going"	10	4	6	3
"College retention"	20	14	20+	12
"Full equalization"	13	6	8	6

SOURCE: RAND Education Simulation Model.

that must be dealt with is the fact that the making of the investments and the accruing of benefits do not overlap in time: the investments are concentrated in the early years of a cohort while the benefits accrue only after an individual's education is completed and are spread over that individual's lifetime. Taxpayers may be reluctant to support such increases in educational investments because they may perceive that the future benefits will accrue not to them but to the next generation. Our showing that the costs of closing the educational attainment gap may be recouped within a decade or so—and thus well within the lifetime of most of those called upon to make the investment—provides a strong argument that indeed the investment is in the taxpayers' self-interest as well.

In this chapter, we considered four alternative goals for closing the educational attainment gap between blacks and Hispanics, on one hand, and non-Hispanic whites, on the other. Each goal, if met, would make a different contribution to reducing this gap and to increasing the overall educational attainment of the labor force. In addition, each would have its own school and college enrollment and cost implications. Table 5.5 compares the effects each goal would have on the six outcomes of interest outlined earlier in this chapter. The table also compares these alternatives using a simple scoring system (bottom panel). Scores on each outcome range from 1 (lowest) to 4 (highest); goals that differ only slightly from one another on a specific outcome are assigned the same score. The goal that decreases the gap in education the most is scored the highest, as is the goal that increases the educational level of the labor force the most. On the enrollment and cost outcomes, the goal with the lowest costs is scored the highest. Note that, as we discussed earlier, even if the costs of meeting these goals actually differ from our projected estimates, the relative ranking of our four goals would not be altered. Indeed, to the extent that excess capacity already exists in the system, it is more likely to affect those goals with the lowest increase in enrollment, and thus will decrease the costs of those goals relative to goals that require a large increase in enrollment. Similarly, if additional services are needed to keep blacks and Hispanics in school or college, the additional costs incurred are likely to be the lowest for goals that intervene at one level of education, and the highest for those requiring intervention at two or more levels.

Table 5.5

Comparing the Outcomes of Alternative Goals for Closing the Educational Attainment Gap Between Non-Hispanic Whites and Blacks and Mexicans, California

Goals	Reduced Gap[a] (percent)				Percent Increase in Educational Attainment of Labor Force		Percent Increase in FTE Enrollment			Percent Increase in Costs	Public Cost/ Benefit Ratio	Years to Break Even
	Some College		College Graduate									
	Black	Mexican	Black	Mexican	Some College	College Grad.	High School	Lower Division	Upper Division			
"High school"	−75	−40	−35	−17	11	9	5	14	14	9	2.4	8
"College-going"	−100	−81	−37	−33	−21	17	5	26	25	15	2.1	10
"College retention"	0	0	−44	−22	0	10	0	1	5	3	1.4	20+
"Full equalization"	−100	−81	−96	−81	21	38	5	28	35	21	1.9	13
					Rank Scores							
"High school"	2	2	1	1	2	1	1	3	3	3	4	4
"College-going"	4	4	2	3	4	3	1	2	2	2	3	3
"College retention"	1	1	3	2	1	2	4	4	4	4	1	1
"Full equalization"	4	4	4	4	4	4	1	1	1	1	2	2

SOURCE: RAND Education Simulation Model.

[a]Reduction in the difference between the share of blacks and Mexicans and the share of non-Hispanic whites completing the same level of education.

Meeting the "full equalization" goal would contribute the most to closing the gap. It fully closes the gap in college-going and college graduation (96 percent) for blacks and closes most of that gap (80 percent) for Hispanics. For the latter, immigration is what keeps the gap in college-going and completion from being fully closed. This goal also significantly increases—by nearly 40 percent—the share of the labor force with a college education: nearly one-third of it would be college graduates, compared to one-quarter in 1990. However, this goal requires a nearly one-third increase in college enrollment and is the most expensive of the goals. Also, it is not the goal with the highest benefit/cost ratio.

The "high school" goal has the highest benefit/cost ratio. Its achievement requires about half the expansion in college FTE enrollment required for the "full equalization" goal, and it is about two times less expensive. It significantly reduces the gap in the share of blacks and Hispanics having some college—by 75 and 40 percent, respectively. However, it contributes the least of the four goals to reducing the gap in college graduates.

Somewhat more effective in reducing the gap in the share of college graduates is the "college retention" goal. But this goal contributes nothing to reducing the gap in the share of those with some college. And although it is the least expensive of all four goals, it also has the lowest benefit/cost ratio: the savings in public expenditures and the gain in tax revenues produced by increasing an individual's education from some college to college graduate are low relative to the gains made by increasing an individual's education from high school dropout to high school graduate (see Chapter Three).

Finally, achievement of the "college-going" goal would contribute as much as achievement of the "full equalization" goal to eliminating the gap in the share of those with some college. However, it would contribute about two-thirds less to reducing the gap in college graduates and one-half less to increasing the share of college graduates in the labor force. This goal requires a one-fourth increase in FTE college enrollment and is the second most expensive. Its benefit/cost ratio is lower than that of the "high school" goal but higher than that of the "full equalization" goal.

What becomes clear from this discussion is that none of the four goals considered is clearly preferable to the others. Each involves making trade-offs between gap reduction, costs, and public benefits. In choosing which goal to pursue, one cannot avoid weighing the relative importance of the differences in contributions to the various outcomes. If maximizing closure of the gap in college-going and college completion between ethnic groups is most important, setting a "full equalization" goal may be preferred. If minimizing the expansion of educational institutions and costs is most important, setting a goal similar to our "college retention" may be preferred. If maximizing public returns on public investments is most important, focusing on equalizing high school graduation rates, our "high school" goal, may be preferred. And if obtaining a relative balance between the various outcomes is most important, the "college-going" goal may be preferred.

The analyses discussed in this chapter yielded two additional insights that deserve highlighting here. The first is that success in closing the educational attainment gap between blacks and Hispanics and non-Hispanic whites may result in increased differentials in the educational attainment of the labor force between regions or states. This result stems from the large variations in the concentration of blacks and Hispanics in different states and differentials in educational transition probabilities among states.

A second insight yielded by our analyses is that a reduction in the educational attainment gap between ethnic groups may increase the educational attainment gap between native-borns and immigrants. This is because a large share of immigrants enter the country as adults with a relatively low level of education and only minimally acquire additional education in the United States. How immigration affects the context and demand for education is examined in the next chapter.

Chapter Six

EFFECTS OF IMMIGRATION ON EDUCATION

The changes in immigration policy enacted by Congress in the 1965 Immigration and Naturalization Act are at the roots of today's rapid changes in the ethnic composition of the nation's population. The number of immigrants allowed to enter the United States was increased, the national origin quotas that favored European immigration were abolished, and the door was opened to immigration from Asia and eventually Latin America. In addition, the preference for immigration of family members, including extended family members, was expanded.[1] At the same time, Congress terminated the agricultural temporary worker ("Bracero") program, an act that eventually led to a predominantly legal and seasonal flow of Mexican immigrants turning into a predominantly illegal and permanent flow. These changes were followed in the 1970s and 1980s by an inflow of refugees from Cuba, the former Soviet Union, and Southeast Asia; by the legalization, in 1986, of 2.6 million undocumented immigrants nationwide through the amnesty provisions of the Immigration Reform and Control Act (IRCA); and by a further 40 percent expansion, in 1990, in the number of immigrants allowed to enter the country permanently every year.

Currently, in excess of 1 million new immigrants settle permanently in the country every year, the overwhelming majority of whom are from Asia and Latin America, including Mexico.

---

[1]Because family reunification remained the cornerstone of U.S. immigration policy, Congress did not anticipate that the changes being made would, over time, significantly alter the distribution of immigrants by country of origin.

Cumulatively, these changes have affected the pattern of immigration in two significant ways that are particularly relevant to our study of trends in educational attainment. First, the number of immigrants in the population has increased rapidly and is continuing to do so. In the 1990s, immigrants have been contributing in excess of one-third to the growth of the nation's labor force, and all of the growth of California's labor force (Vernez, 1999). Second, the educational attainment of recent immigrants, although higher than that of immigrants who came in earlier years, has declined relative to that of native-borns. For instance, whereas in 1970 immigrants were 30 percent more likely than native-borns to have fewer than 12 years of education (50 vs. 38 percent), in 1990 they were 130 percent more likely (30 vs. 13 percent). Immigrants and native-borns, however, have remained just as likely to be college graduates.[2]

In brief, immigrants are increasingly playing a dominant role in determining the overall educational attainment of the nation's population and hence the quality of its labor force. In this chapter, we examine how dominant this role is by exploring how changes in immigration policy would affect the demand for education and the overall distribution of educational attainment.

In the previous chapter, we held immigration patterns constant—set at the volume and composition prevailing in the 1985–1990 period—while we explored the effects of various ways in which the educational attainment gap between non-Hispanic whites, on one hand, and blacks and Hispanics, on the other, might be reduced. In this chapter, we do the reverse: we hold educational transition rates constant—set at the levels prevailing in the early 1990s—and explore the effects of changes in immigration.[3] The two alternative changes in immigration policy that we consider are introduced first, after which we discuss the effect that a change in the volume of immigration would have on the size and ethnic composition of the population. The last section of the chapter compares the effects of the two

---

[2]These figures are for persons in the labor force at the time of the 1970 and 1990 U.S. Census of Population.

[3]The relative effects of changes in immigration policy with respect to each one of the four educational goals discussed in Chapter Five would be similar to those discussed here relative to a continuation of current educational attainment.

alternative changes on the demand for and costs of education, the educational attainment of minorities, and the population as a whole.

ALTERNATIVE IMMIGRATION POLICIES

The size and composition of the annual flows of immigrants considered in our previous analyses were those that prevailed during the 1985–1990 period. Some 930,000 new immigrants were added annually to the nation's population, of whom 29 percent were Asian, 6 percent were black, 28 percent were Mexican, 18 percent were Other Hispanic, and 20 percent were non-Hispanic white. The majority (70 percent) of these immigrants were adults; the balance were children and youths age 17 or younger. With regard to educational attainment of the adult immigrants, one-third had less than a high school education, 20 percent had a high school education only, 11 percent had some college, and 16 percent had a bachelor's degree or more.

As noted earlier, the volume of immigration in the 1990s has exceeded the 1985–1990 level, reaching about 1 million yearly. Moreover, the share of Mexican immigrants in this flow has increased at the expense of non-Hispanics. Over the 1990–1997 period, 30 percent of immigrants entering the labor market were Mexican and 17 percent were Other Hispanic. Asians maintained their share at 28 percent, as did blacks at 7 percent, but the share of non-Hispanic whites declined to 13 percent. What these numbers suggest is that our estimates of the effects of changes in immigration policies may be understated.

In the 1990s, the growing volume of immigrants and the country's inability to effectively stem illegal immigration have led to calls for implementing changes in immigration policy. Some people have called for a moratorium on new immigration or a significant decrease in the annual number of immigrants—down to 200,000 or fewer yearly—permitted to enter the country (Federation for American Immigration Reform, 1994). Others have called for changes that would put greater emphasis on the needs of the economy while limiting the primacy of family reunification to nuclear, rather than extended, family members (U.S. Commission on Immigration Reform, 1997; McCarthy and Vernez, 1997; Papademetriou and Yale-Loehr, 1996). These latter proposed changes are directed at moderating the volume of immigration and at giving greater, although *not* exclusive, weight to the level of education of would-be immigrants.

To explore how immigration policy affects population growth and, in turn, educational institutions, we considered the following two extreme policies:

1. *No immigration.* This "no immigration" policy assumes a virtual closing of U.S. borders to permanent immigration beginning with the year 2000. In other words, no new immigrants would be added to the U.S. population from the year 2000 on. Immigration through the 1990s remains at the level and of the composition described for the base case.

2. *Curb on permanent immigration of people with fewer than 12 years of education.* For this "no dropouts" policy, no immigrants with fewer than 12 years of education would be permitted to permanently settle in the United States beginning with the year 2000. The annual volume of immigration remains as in the base case, and immigrants with fewer than 12 years of education are replaced by immigrants with higher levels of education in proportion to their relative size in the base case. The age and ethnic distributions of immigrants also remain as in the base case.

These two alternatives are extremes. Few, if any, are advocating closing our borders to all newcomers who want to settle permanently in the United States; just as few, if any, are advocating excluding all low-educated persons from immigration. The justification for our exploring these alternatives in this first effort to measure the long-term effects of immigration policy is that they clearly display the maximum range (sensitivities) of effects of potential policy changes.

EFFECTS ON SIZE AND COMPOSITION OF POPULATION

Figure 6.1 compares the projected size of the cohort born in 1990 at age 40 (i.e., in the year 2030) under our immigration base case (i.e., current immigration) and zero immigration beginning in 2000. The reader should keep in mind that under the "no immigration" alternative, immigration during the first ten years of the life of the cohort (i.e., from 1990 to 1999) continues at the same level and ethnic composition as in the base case.

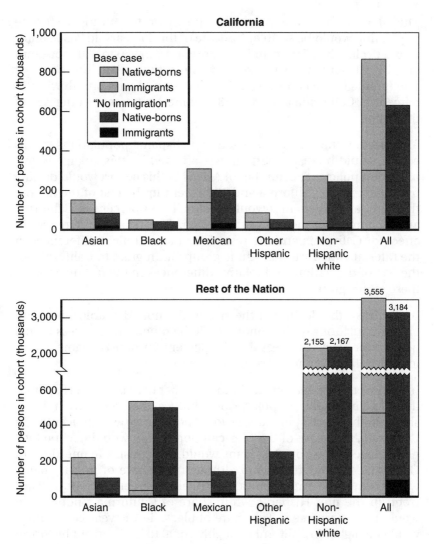

SOURCE: RAND Education Simulation Model.

Figure 6.1—Effects of "No Immigration" Policy on Size of 1990-Born Cohort at Age 40, California and Rest of the Nation

The effect of the "no immigration" policy on the future size of the population would be sizable. The size of the 40-year-old 2030 cohort would decline by 27 percent in California (from 860 to 630 thousand) and by 10 percent in the rest of the nation. And the share of immigrants in the cohort would decline from nearly one-third to 14 percent in California and from 13 to a mere 3 percent in the rest of the nation.

As expected, the size of the Asian and Hispanic populations in this cohort would be disproportionately affected by this change in im-migration policy. The number of Asians in this cohort would decline by 44 percent in California and 49 percent in the rest of the nation; the number of Hispanics would decline by 34 percent in California and 26 percent in the rest of the nation. The relative differences in effect for California and the rest of the nation reflect differences in the rates at which various ethnic groups immigrate to California vs. the rest of the nation, and relative differences in the fertility rates of these ethnic groups.

By contrast, the decline in the size of the non-Hispanic white and black populations in the cohort would be much smaller: less than 5 percent for blacks and less than 10 percent for non-Hispanic whites in both California and the rest of the nation.

In spite of the sizable decline in the number of Asians and Hispanics that a "no immigration" policy would induce, their respective relative shares in the overall population would not change as significantly. In California, the share of the Mexican population would decline by 3 percentage points, but Mexicans would still constitute one-third of California's population. And although the share of non-Hispanic whites would be larger, 38 rather than 31 percent, the downward trend in the non-Hispanic white share of California's population would not be reversed. The share of blacks in the year 2030 cohort would be higher in California, roughly equal to its 7 percent historical level instead of declining to 5 percent.

The effect of "zero immigration" in the rest of the nation would be similar to that in California, although on a smaller scale. The largest effect would be on the share of Hispanics, which would decline from 16 to 13 percent. Non-Hispanic whites would increase their share from 64 to 68 percent.

The main point to retain from this analysis is that closing U.S. borders to permanent immigration would somewhat slow the shifts in the ethnic composition of the U.S. population but would not alter it dramatically in the long term. The 30 years of cumulatively higher immigration from Asia and Latin America beginning in the late 1960s and the (at least currently) higher fertility rates for Hispanics and some Asians than for non-Hispanic whites are assuring that the nation's and California's ethnic compositional change will continue.

A word of caution, however. The ethnic groupings used in our analysis are based on today's reported ethnic self-identity. There is no telling how the ongoing increase in marriage between members of different ethnic groups may affect current ethnic identities. It may well blur them or it may strengthen them, possibly more for some ethnic groups than for others. Whatever the outcome, this process is likely to be stronger under a "no immigration" policy than under a maintenance of current policy, which year after year will bring new Asian and Hispanic immigrants, thereby helping to maintain today's ethnic distinctions.

EFFECTS ON EDUCATIONAL INSTITUTIONS

Under the "no immigraton" policy, FTE enrollment in educational institutions would be reduced by an overall 9 percent in California and by more than 3 percent in the rest of the nation, accounting for about one-fourth of the increase in total enrollment that would otherwise be required to meet our projected growth in the national school-age population (see Chapter One). Colleges and universities would be more affected than high schools (Figure 6.2). For instance, in California, enrollment would be reduced by 7 percent in the high schools, compared to 10 percent in lower-division and 12 percent in upper-division college. Notably, graduate enrollment (not shown in Figure 6.2) would be reduced the most, by more than one-fifth in California and nearly one-sixth in the rest of the nation.

By contrast, changing the educational composition of immigrants— the "no dropouts" option—would increase FTE enrollment, albeit only slightly. Overall, enrollment would increase by less than 2 percent in California and less than 1 percent in the rest of the nation. Again, the distribution of the change in enrollment would vary across levels of education. There would be a slight decline in enrollment in the nation's high schools. But enrollment would increase at the postsecondary levels by about 4 percent in California and 1 percent in the rest of the nation.

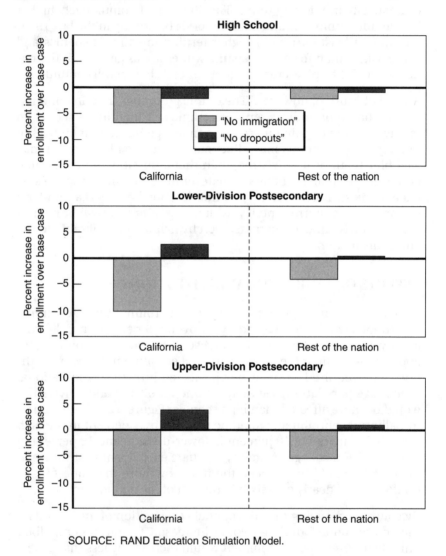

SOURCE: RAND Education Simulation Model.

Figure 6.2—Change in FTE Enrollment Under Alternative Immigration Policies Relative to Base Case, California and Rest of the Nation

Figure 6.3 displays the effects that the immigration policy alternatives would have on the costs of education. The effects would be the greatest in California, where a "no immigration" policy would reduce education costs by more than 10 percent, and a "no dropout" policy would add about 2 percent to state educational costs. In the rest of the nation, cost savings under the "no immigration" policy would be half of those in California, while the added costs of the "no dropouts" policy would be insignificant.

EFFECTS ON DISTRIBUTION OF EDUCATIONAL ATTAINMENT

The considered changes in immigration policy would significantly affect the overall educational distribution of the labor force over the long term in California, but would not have as much of an effect in the rest of the nation (Figure 6.4). If no new immigrants entered California after the year 2000, the share of high school dropouts at age 40 in the 1990-born cohort would decline by 42 percent as the

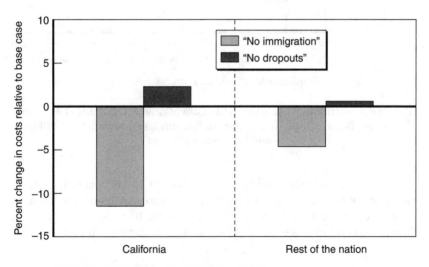

SOURCE: RAND Education Simulation Model.

Figure 6.3—Change in Educational Costs Under Alternative Immigration Policies Relative to Base Case, California and Rest of the Nation

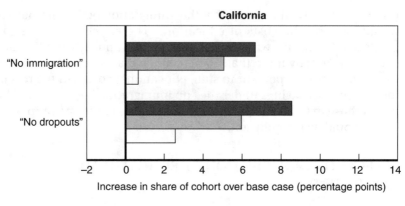

Increase in share of cohort over base case (percentage points)

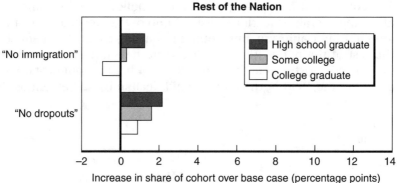

Increase in share of cohort over base case (percentage points)

SOURCE: RAND Education Simulation Model.

Figure 6.4—Estimated Changes in the Educational Attainment at Age 40 of the Cohort Born in 1990 Under Alternative Immigration Policies, California and Rest of the Nation

share of high school graduates rose from 9 to 16 percent, or by 7 percentage points. And the share of the cohort with some college or more would increase by 5 percentage points, from 59 to 64 percent. The share of college graduates, however, would increase only slightly.

Similarly, the "no dropouts" policy would reduce the share of California's high school dropouts by half as the share of high school graduates rose from 7 to 16 percent. The share of those with some college would increase by 6 percentage points, to 65 percent, and there would be a nonnegligible increase in the share of college graduates, 2.5 percentage points.

One way to gauge the relative significance of these effects is to compare them to the effects of meeting the four educational goals considered in Chapter Five (see, especially, Figure 5.3). A "no immigration" or "no dropouts" immigration policy would reduce the share of dropouts and increase the share of college-educated persons in California in the same proportion as would the "high school" goal for education—i.e., a policy that successfully equalized the high school graduation rates of blacks and Hispanics with those of non-Hispanic whites. And a "no dropouts" immigration policy would result in the same increase in the share of college graduates as an education policy that successfully equalized high school graduation rates ("high school" goal) or college retention rates ("college retention" goal).

The effects of a change in immigration policy, even as extreme as the alternatives considered here, however, would not be as sizable in the rest of the nation as they are in California (Figure 6.4). Whereas a "no immigration" policy would reduce the share of dropouts in California by 42 percent, it would reduce this share by 10 percent in the rest of the nation. And it would have no sizable effect on the share of the cohort with some college or with college degrees. The estimated effects of the "no dropouts" option on these shares are more sizable, but they are about four times lower than those in California. And in contrast to the case for California, these effects are somewhat lower than those for the educational goals considered in Chapter Five (again, compare Figures 6.4 and 5.3).

Two factors contribute to these differentials of change in immigration policy between California and the rest of the nation: the significantly higher relative volume of and the higher share of low-educated immigrants in California than in the rest of the nation.

The gap in educational attainment between Hispanics (but not blacks) and non-Hispanic whites is also affected by immigration policy. In California, a "no immigration" policy would reduce the gap in the share of high school graduates by nearly half for both Mexicans and Other Hispanics (Figure 6.5). It would also reduce the gap

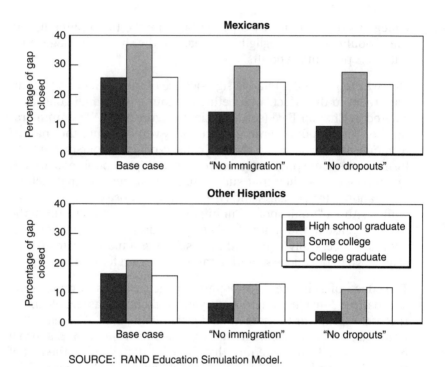

SOURCE: RAND Education Simulation Model.

Figure 6.5—Percentage of Gap in Educational Attainment Closed for Hispanics Under Alternative Immigration Policies, by Level of Education, California

in those with some college—especially for Other Hispanics—but would have only a relatively minor effect on reducing the gap in the share of college graduates.

Excluding immigrants with fewer than 12 years of education—the "no dropouts" policy—would have an even greater impact. In California, it would close two-thirds of the gap in the share of high school graduates between non-Hispanic whites and Mexicans, and three-quarters of that gap for Other Hispanics. It would also halve the gap in the share of those with some college between non-Hispanic whites and Other Hispanics, but would close only one-quarter of that gap for Mexicans.[4]

In the rest of the nation, the alternative immigration policies considered here would do as much to reduce the gap in educational attainment between non-Hispanic whites and Mexicans as they do in California. However, the gap-reducing effect for Other Hispanics would be significantly lower than in California. Indeed, the "no immigration" policy would do nothing to reduce the gap between non-Hispanic whites and Other Hispanics in the rest of the nation. And the "no dropouts" policy would have about half the reducing effect on the share of both high school graduates and those with some college that it would have in California. One reason for this difference is that the educational attainment of native-born Other Hispanics is significantly lower in the rest of the nation than it is in California.[5]

The changes in immigration policies considered here would not close as much of the education gap between non-Hispanic whites and Hispanics and blacks as would the education alternatives considered in Chapter Five (compare Figures 5.1 and 6.5), most especially with regard to reducing the gap in both the share of those with some college and the share of college graduates. However, the reverse is true with regard to reducing the gap in the share of high school graduates. This gap would be reduced more by a "no immigration" or "no dropout" immigration policy than by meeting any of the educational goals considered. These findings underline the significant effect of immigration policy on the distribution of educational attainment, most particularly at the lower end of the educational distribution.

CONCLUSIONS

The desirability of the current level and educational composition of immigrants continues to be a subject of national debate. The current

---

[4]Because the number of blacks immigrating to the United States is small relative to the number of native-born blacks, a change in immigration policy would have no significant effect on the educational attainment gap between blacks and non-Hispanic whites.

[5]A large share of native-born Other Hispanics in the rest of the nation are of Puerto Rican origin, a group having a relatively low level of educational attainment.

high volume of immigrants, a sizable share of whom have a low level of education, is significantly affecting not only the future size of the nation's population, but its overall educational attainment as well. The high volume is also affecting the demand for and costs of education. High immigration states, such as California, are disproportionately affected.

To size up the effect of immigration on education, we considered two extreme departures from current immigration (our base case) policy: a "no immigration" and a "no dropouts" immigration policy starting with the year 2000. We found that a "no immigration" policy would decrease FTE enrollment and education costs (relative to our base case) by about 10 percent in California and 5 percent in the rest of the nation. In contrast, a "no dropouts" policy, restricting immigration to those with at least 12 years of education while maintaining the same volume of immigration, would increase education costs, but only marginally.

Immigration policy also affects the educational attainment of the labor force. Compared to current immigration policy, a "no immigration" or a "no dropouts" policy would cut the share of high school dropouts in the California labor force by about 50 percent and increase the share with some college by 10 percent. The "no dropouts" policy would also increase the share of college graduates in the labor force by 10 percent. These effects would be much smaller, however, in the rest of the nation.

As for the gap in educational attainment between non-Hispanic whites and blacks and Hispanics, we found that both immigration policies considered would reduce the gap in the share of high school graduates between Hispanics and non-Hispanic whites by 50 percent or more in both California and the rest of the nation. There would be no effect, however, on the educational attainment gap between blacks and non-Hispanic whites.

Finally, as compared to current policy, a "no immigration" policy would slow down the rate of change in the ethnic composition of the population but would not significantly alter the long-term outcome. The immigration that has taken place over the past 30 years and the higher fertility rates of Hispanics and some Asians compared to other groups assure that the shift in the ethnic composition of the nation's population will continue, even without further immigration.

Chapter Seven

DISCUSSION AND NEXT STEPS

We have shown that closing the educational attainment gap between blacks and Hispanics, on one hand, and non-Hispanic whites, on the other, can more than pay for itself in the form of both reduced public expenditures on social transfer programs and added tax revenues throughout the lifetime of the beneficiaries. Indeed, the added costs of providing more education may be recouped within a relatively short period of ten to 15 years, well within the lifetime of most taxpayers called upon to make the investments. Closing the gap would, however, require that the capacity of the education system be expanded, most particularly in high-immigration states. In California, for instance, to equalize the college-going and college-completion rates of blacks and Hispanics to those of non-Hispanic whites would require a one-third increase in FTE enrollment in postsecondary educational institutions. This expansion would be in addition to that required to meet a projected 20 percent or greater increase in the number of youths of college age between now and 2015. The expansion required in the rest of the nation would be smaller, however.

Immigration is the main reason for the profoundly changed demographic and social context facing educational institutions. Since the early 1970s, increasingly higher numbers of immigrants have fueled the rapid ethnic compositional shift that is taking place in California and, more slowly, in the rest of the nation. Blacks and Hispanics now account for a majority of youths entering school in California and about 30 percent in the rest of the nation. Immigration has also contributed significantly to the large gap in educational attainment between Hispanics and non-Hispanic whites.

A reduction in future immigration or a shift in its composition toward better-educated immigrants would only somewhat alleviate future demands on educational institutions. For instance, if there were no further immigration beginning with year 2000, FTE enrollment and educational costs would decrease by about 10 percent in California and 5 percent in the rest of the nation. This "no immigration" policy or a policy limiting permanent entry to immigrants with at least a high school education while maintaining the current number of immigrants (as some have advocated) would cut the gap in the share of high school graduates between Hispanics and non-Hispanic whites by half. However, changes in immigration policy would have no effect on the gap between blacks and non-Hispanic whites. And regardless of any changes that may be made in years to come, the immigration that has taken place over the past 30 years and the high fertility rates among Hispanics are assuring a continuation of the ethnic shift of the nation's population.

As a result, the education challenge for California—and to a lesser extent the rest of the nation—brought about by the rapid changes that have taken place over the past 25 years is clearly daunting. But the price of not confronting it may be even greater. Failure to increase the educational attainment of Hispanics and blacks will lead to growing shares of new entrants into the labor force having lower levels of educational attainment than those that prevail today—and at the very time when at least one or more years of postsecondary education has become a prerequisite for competing in the U.S. economy and commanding a living wage. This failure will also lead to a further increase in the educational gap between blacks and Hispanics, on the one hand, and Asians and non-Hispanic whites, on the other hand, thereby creating a potentially volatile social environment. And as we have shown, this failure would lead to significantly higher public expenditures for social and health programs for generations to come.

In our analysis, we considered the educational benefits, institutional costs, and public benefits of meeting four alternative goals designed to reduce the educational attainment gap between Hispanics and blacks and non-Hispanic whites. Each of these alternatives entails intervening at different points in the educational process, and each involves making trade-offs among the benefits that may eventually accrue to the public at large, the costs of providing the additional education, and the resulting distribution of educational attainment across ethnic groups and overall.

We found that a focus just on equalizing the high school graduation rates of ethnic groups would produce the highest public benefits-to-costs ratio but would contribute the least to reducing the gaps in shares of college graduates. To maximize gap reduction in the shares of college graduates would require a focus on equalizing not only high school graduation rates but college-going and college-retention rates as well. But this goal's accomplishment would increase FTE enrollment by one-third in California and about 12 percent in the rest of the nation, and it is the most expensive. Alternatively, a focus on equalizing college retention rates for ethnic groups would do as much to reduce the gap in the shares of college graduates as would a focus on equalizing high school graduation rates, and it would be the least expensive of the goals considered. But it would also have the lowest long-term public return. Finally, if maintaining a balance between educational benefits, institutional costs, and public returns is preferred, focusing on equalizing high school graduation rates and the college-going rates of these graduates might be the preferred goal of those we considered.

For every alternative goal considered, we estimated that the long-term benefits in the form of savings in public expenditures for social and health programs and increased tax revenues would exceed the costs of providing the additional education. Our benefit estimates are approximations using early 1990s public program participation, benefit costs, and earnings by level of education. In other words, they do not account for potential changes in the relationships among these items over time. Similarly, our cost estimates assume mid-1990s average costs. They thus do not account for the fact that while some states may have excess capacity that could lower actual costs, other states may be experiencing overcrowding that could require major new capital expenditures and thus increase actual costs. Even though our assumptions may alter the magnitude of our estimates, they should not bias the relative ordering of the costs and benefits of the goals considered.

Setting a goal and showing that, if met, it would more than pay for it-self is but a first step.[1] Meeting this goal is another thing. To this end, several issues remain to be addressed.

One issue is the incentive that states have to invest less in education than may be optimal, most particularly in postsecondary education. As we have demonstrated, states can significantly alter the distribution of the educational attainment of their labor force through both internal and international migration. Hence, a state that does not produce enough college graduates to meet its labor force demands can import them from another state or another nation at no immediate cost to it. The other side of the coin is that a state that produces a large number of college graduates may not capture the full benefits from that investment. The size of this phenomenon is not insignificant and is a strong argument for the federal government to play a leading role in promoting and funding efforts to close the education gap for blacks and Hispanics. This is all the more so because the responsibility to educate these minorities falls to a handful of states—California, Florida, New York, Illinois, and Texas.

Another issue is know-how. Increasing the educational attainment of blacks and Hispanics may require implementing targeted programs designed to support and promote the educational persistence and achievement of these minorities on a much larger scale than is currently the case. The design of such large-scale programs will have to be based on a better understanding of the complex reasons why individuals fail to persist in their education. Indeed, it appears that in spite of the multitude of demonstration programs and other activities that have been implemented to help minority students, there still is no consensus on when, where, and how to intervene on a systemwide scale to effectively change past patterns of relatively low educational attainment. One reason is that the key factors that may explain the lagging educational performance of blacks and Hispanics—and other minorities—are not well understood.

---

[1]While we have focused on the public benefits of increased education for blacks and Hispanics, others have documented the private monetary as well as nonmonetary effects of a postsecondary education, including how it affects psychological well-being, quality of life, and civic participation. For instance, see Pascarella and Terenzini, 1991, for a comprehensive review of studies treating college effects on students. Also, Bowen and Bok (1998) document the positive effects of a college education on earnings, civic participation, and satisfaction with life.

Factors that have been associated with the relatively low educational performance of Hispanics fall into four categories: school based, parent based, cultural, and structural/institutional. Different studies have typically emphasized one or more of these factors, but which dominate and, among these, which can be effectively acted upon remain uncertain.

School-based factors were emphasized by the President's Advisory Commission on Educational Excellence for Hispanic Americans (1996), including such disparate factors as inequity in school financing, school segregation and poverty, lack of bilingual and English as a Second Language (ESL) programs, underutilization of technology, underrepresentation of Hispanics among school personnel, misplacement of students in special education classes, testing and assessment, and lack of school safety. The disadvantages of Hispanic children relative to these factors are well documented in the Advisory Commission's report. What is not known, however, is the relative contribution of each of these factors to educational achievement or attainment. Additional and/or reallocation of resources can address some of these factors; however, past attempts at desegregation have been impaired by stubbornly segregated residential patterns by class and ethnicity. And school finance reform efforts—many court ordered—do not seem to have had the hoped-for results in correcting resource allocation inequities. Also, some of the school-based factors are not readily amenable to remedies, at least not in the short term. For instance, it will take a generation or more to alleviate the underrepresentation of Hispanic teachers in the nation's classrooms.

By contrast, parental/family factors have been consistently found to be associated with the educational achievement and educational attainment of all ethnic groups, all else being equal (Vernez and Abrahamse, 1996; Grissmer et al., 1994; Hill and O'Neill, 1993; Hanushek, 1992; Blake, 1989). Two factors in particular stand out in these studies: family income and level of education of the father and mother. Hispanic and black children are more likely than other groups of children to be disadvantaged in terms of these factors (Vernez and Abrahamse, 1996). Family size is another factor that has been associated with educational attainment, and, as noted above, Hispanic children are more likely to live in large families than are other children. All three of these factors measure different dimensions of a family's monetary resources and the parental know-how, time, and attention it can devote in support of a child's education. Income assistance programs can alleviate the income gaps between Hispanics and other groups. But public funding for these programs is being reduced at the same time college tuition and fees are going up. By 1994, tuition and fees had risen by more than 100 percent in real terms compared to those in 1976 (Commission on National Investment in Higher Education, 1997). Also, low levels of parental education are not readily amenable to change, and how to compensate for disadvantages due to lack of access to this most important parental resource is an unresolved question. An expansion of after-school programs coupled with intensive tutoring may be one approach, but the effectiveness of such programs, as is true for most options, is yet to be rigorously determined.

Several studies suggest that the significance of race/ethnicity persists in explaining school performance—even after controlling for social class, family structure, and parental education (e.g., Steinberg, 1996; Vernez and Abrahamse, 1996; Portes and Rumbaut, 1996)—with Asians outperforming all others and Hispanics lagging all others. Two additional sets of factors have been offered to explain the pattern of lower educational attainment for blacks and Hispanics, and for Mexican-origin Hispanics in particular. One set includes cultural factors that place different values on education and, in turn, may affect the motivations and educational expectations of children. However, several authors have pointed out the paradox of a positive attitude toward education—which Hispanics have been found to possess at a high level, although seemingly not at as high a level as other groups—being associated with low performance in school (e.g., Mickelson, 1990). One explanation for this paradox is that this attitude is affected by what is learned from daily experience and reality. Children and adolescents see their parents' experiences in a labor market in which class and other factors influence the return on education (Mickelson, 1990). This explanation is linked to structural/institutional labor market and societal factors—the second set of factors—that may affect students' perceptions of what is possible: over time and subsequent generations, the children of minority immigrants may increasingly perceive that their opportunities are limited, which reduces their sense and value of education (Ogbu, 1991).

Which of these factors, individually or in combination, explain the relatively low educational attainment of Hispanics needs to be determined if the education of the nation's Hispanic children is to be effectively upgraded. Regardless, however, two things appear to be certain. First, closing the gap in the educational attainment of blacks and Hispanics will require intervening beyond the classroom and probably will require experimenting with more involvement of parents and communities. Second, such an effort will have to be sustained over the long term.

The costs of implementing such programs will be in addition to those we have estimated in the effort described in this report. But, as we have shown, the nation could invest up to twice the average cost per FTE on minorities and still recoup this investment over the life of the beneficiaries.

A third issue concerns convincing the public that the investment will actually result in increased educational attainment for blacks and Hispanics. After decades of increased expenditures in education, little progress has been made in reducing the gap in college-going and college completion between ethnic groups (see Chapter One). If renewed efforts are made, they must be closely monitored and evaluated for effectiveness. An associated obstacle is the growing public suspicion of programs that take ethnicity into account, such as affirmative action. Already, three states—California, Texas, and Washington—no longer permit ethnicity to be a factor in admitting students to college. Alternative programs will have to be developed if the gap in educational attainment is to be closed rather than enlarged.

DATA USED TO ESTIMATE PUBLIC PROGRAM BENEFITS

This appendix provides further details on the data used to estimate the public program benefits received by individuals, as discussed in Chapter Two.

PROGRAM UTILIZATION RATES

Table A.1 displays the utilization rates by ethnic group and by educational attainment for each of the programs considered in this study and as measured by the U.S. Bureau of the Census's 1990 and 1991 panels of the Survey of Income and Program Participation (SIPP). Of the 58,000 observations age 18 or older in the panel for all of 1991, approximately 54 percent are female. Just under 79 percent of the sample are non-Hispanic white; non-Hispanic blacks make up just under 10 percent. Mexicans are approximately 5 percent of the sample, and Other Hispanics are just under 4 percent. Asians and Pacific Islanders make up the balance. Approximately 10 percent of the sample are immigrants. (Other races—American Indians, Eskimos, and Aleuts—are excluded from the analysis.)

Participation in each program declines substantially as educational attainment increases. This is true across racial/ethnic groups and within each group. Participation in public assistance programs such as welfare, SSI, and Medicaid ranges from 16 percent among high school dropouts to nearly zero among college graduates. For social insurance programs such as Social Security and Medicare, participation rates do not decline as precipitously; among retirees, eligibility

Table A.1

1991 Program Utilization Rates Among Adults, by Educational Attainment

Ethnicity	Less Than High School Graduate	High School Graduate	Some College	Bachelor's Degree or More
Welfare (AFDC, General Assistance, and/or Other Welfare)				
Non-Hispanic white	4.5	2.5	1.7	0.3
Black	15.0	11.4	7.2	1.5
Asian	15.1	7.3	3.0	0.9
Mexican	9.9	5.9	2.7	2.0
Other Hispanic	15.2	8.7	4.7	1.6
Total, all groups	7.6	3.8	2.4	0.5
Food Stamps and/or WIC				
Non-Hispanic white	10.8	5.2	3.0	0.7
Black	29.5	19.7	13.1	2.0
Asian	18.4	9.0	3.5	2.2
Mexican	23.5	14.8	7.3	5.4
Other Hispanic	30.9	15.8	8.1	3.5
Total, all groups	16.4	7.4	4.2	0.9
Federal and State Unemployment Insurance				
Non-Hispanic white	5.8	7.1	5.4	3.8
Black	5.5	8.1	6.1	3.0
Asian	4.6	5.4	4.4	4.8
Mexican	12.2	11.1	8.0	1.3
Other Hispanic	6.0	6.4	8.1	4.3
Total, all groups	6.5	7.3	5.6	3.7
Federal and State Supplemental Security Income				
Non-Hispanic white	6.1	1.5	0.8	0.3
Black	16.0	5.8	2.6	0.3
Asian	10.2	4.6	1.6	1.1
Mexican	7.7	1.8	1.3	0.7
Other Hispanic	14.8	3.0	1.6	0.8
Total, all groups	8.4	2.0	1.0	0.4
School Breakfast and/or Lunch Programs				
Non-Hispanic white	11.4	10.0	7.3	3.2
Black	32.2	35.2	27.8	13.4
Asian	37.8	22.2	14.0	9.3
Mexican	51.5	33.6	24.2	13.4
Other Hispanic	34.1	29.7	20.6	9.1
Total, all groups	21.2	14.2	10.3	4.3

Table A.1 (continued)

Ethnicity	Less Than High School Graduate	High School Graduate	Some College	Bachelor's Degree or More
Low-Income Energy Assistance				
Non-Hispanic white	9.5	4.0	2.2	0.7
Black	19.4	9.3	6.9	2.0
Asian	7.6	3.2	0.9	1.5
Mexican	12.5	7.8	4.4	2.0
Other Hispanic	17.3	8.0	4.0	2.0
Total, all groups	11.7	4.8	2.7	0.9
Social Security				
Non-Hispanic white	49.3	22.8	13.9	11.1
Black	42.7	13.5	9.0	11.2
Asian	17.1	14.1	4.4	3.5
Mexican	17.2	7.4	3.8	4.7
Other Hispanic	26.0	12.2	7.0	8.3
Total, all groups	42.3	20.8	12.6	10.6
Medicare				
Non-Hispanic white	45.0	19.6	12.2	10.6
Black	39.6	10.3	7.1	9.7
Asian	18.4	10.7	4.0	3.3
Mexican	15.2	5.5	3.1	3.4
Other Hispanic	25.5	9.4	6.5	8.3
Total, all groups	38.8	17.6	11.0	10.0
Medicaid				
Non-Hispanic white	12.8	5.0	3.0	0.8
Black	32.4	18.2	11.6	1.8
Asian	27.3	12.2	5.4	2.6
Mexican	22.3	11.3	4.4	2.7
Other Hispanic	34.0	15.2	7.8	3.1
Total, all groups	18.5	7.0	4.1	1.0
In Jail or Prison				
Non-Hispanic white	0.3	0.2	0.1	0.0
Black	2.0	1.7	0.9	0.4
Asian	0.2	0.1	0.1	0.0
Mexican	0.8	0.7	0.4	0.2
Other Hispanic	1.1	0.8	0.5	0.3
Total, all groups	0.7	0.4	0.2	0.1

SOURCES: Calculated from 1990 and 1991 data panels of the Survey of Income and Program Participation, the 1991 Survey of Inmates of State Correctional Facilities, and the 1989 Survey of Inmates of Local Jails.

(and benefits) in these programs increases with educational attainment, because an individual's participation in the labor force and wages (before retirement) are greater at higher levels of educational attainment.

There are also large variations within a level of education across ethnic groups. For instance, among high school graduates, blacks and Other Hispanics are more likely than Asians and Mexicans to use Medicaid services and welfare. But Mexicans are more likely to use school breakfast and lunch programs. And non-Hispanic whites are more likely than any other ethnic group to benefit from Social Security and Medicare.[1]

ESTIMATING THE VALUE OF BENEFITS

As noted above, SIPP contains information on program benefits received for most but not all programs. For Medicaid and Medicare, the value of benefits was calculated using the cost data in the 1992 *Medicaid Statistics* (U.S. Department of Health and Human Services, 1993) and the *1996 Green Book* (U.S. House of Representatives, 1996). For those who received hospital care during the year, the benefit is equal to the average amount spent per beneficiary on inpatient and outpatient care. For those who received only ambulatory care during the year, the benefit is equal to the average amount spent on outpatient care per beneficiary. Table A.2 summarizes the cost of inpatient and outpatient care for Medicare and Medicaid.

These costs were then combined with data on hospitalization rates and frequency of outpatient visits from the SIPP to produce estimates of the value of the Medicare and Medicaid benefits received by each beneficiary. As Table A.3 shows, the average number of doctor visits varies both across ethnic groups and by educational attainment.

For cost per meal of the school breakfast and lunch programs, we used the average cost per meal, as shown in Table A.4. And average annual costs per prisoner were derived as shown in Table A.5.

---

[1]Reasons for differences in public service utilization have been explored in various studies, including Borjas and Hilton, 1995; McCarthy and Vernez, 1997; Vernez, 1999.

Table A.2

Cost per Person of Medicare and Medicaid, 1991

Program	Amount (billions of dollars)	Recipients (millions)	Cost per Person (dollars)
Medicare			
Inpatient care	68.7	6.8	10,089
Outpatient care	45.5	26.4	1,726
Medicaid			
Inpatient care	21.9	5.2	4,204
Outpatient care	24.1	21.4	905

SOURCES: U.S. Department of Health and Human Services, 1993; U.S. House of Representatives, 1996.

Table A.3

Number of Times Native-Born Men and Women Medicaid Recipients Visited or Talked to Doctor or Assistant During the Preceding Year, by Ethnicity and Educational Attainment, 1991

Ethnicity	Less Than High School Graduate	High School Graduate	Some College	Bachelor's Degree or More	All Groups
Native-Born Men					
Non-Hispanic white	9.5	6.9	11.1	11.6	8.9
Black	11.5	5.5	6.0	0.0	9.7
Asian	4.0	0.0	1.0	0.0	2.5
Mexican	16.0	10.3	3.3	0.0	14.0
Other Hispanic	9.2	6.4	5.6	6.0	10.3
Total, all groups	10.5	6.7	10.4	11.3	9.4
Native-Born Women					
Non-Hispanic white	9.2	9.6	9.0	10.2	9.4
Black	9.6	7.8	6.4	6.3	8.6
Asian	7.3	6.3	2.0	0.0	6.6
Mexican	6.4	4.5	6.8	2.0	5.8
Other Hispanic	10.2	10.7	11.7	0.0	10.4
Total, all groups	9.2	8.9	8.3	9.4	9.0

SOURCE: 1990 and 1991 panels of the Survey of Income and Program Participation.

Table A.4

Per-Meal Cost of School Breakfast and Lunch Programs

	Per-Meal Cost of Free Meal	Per-Meal Cost of Reduced-Price Meal
School breakfast program	$1.66	$1.26
School lunch program	$0.93	$0.63

SOURCE: U.S. House of Representatives, 1996.

Table A.5

Cost of Incarceration in the United States, 1992

Type of Incarceration	U.S. Corrections System		
	Annual Expenditure (millions of dollars)	Average Daily Number of Prisoners	Annual Cost per Prisoner (1992 $)
State prison	18,751	743,556	25,218
County and municipal jail	10,299	441,889	23,307
Total	29,050	1,185,445	24,496

SOURCE: Maguire and Pastore, 1995.

NOTE: In the model, the annual cost per prisoner was adjusted to 1997 dollars using the CPI: $28,195 total annual cost per prisoner.

ESTIMATED RELATIONSHIPS BETWEEN EDUCATIONAL ATTAINMENT AND SPENDING ON SOCIAL PROGRAMS

This appendix first provides details on the procedures used to estimate the effect of education on public program use and spending. It then provides the results of our estimated models for each of ten families of public programs.

OVERVIEW OF THE TWO-PART MODEL

We first discuss the technique used to estimate the income received from public assistance and social insurance programs other than Medicare and Medicaid. We then discuss the model used to estimate the value of the Medicare and Medicaid benefits.

Estimating Public Assistance and Social Insurance Income

Because only a fraction of the population receives income from public assistance and social insurance income programs, the expected value of the benefits received is divided into two pieces: (1) the probability of receiving public assistance or social insurance income, and (2) the expected value of the benefit, conditional on utilization of the program. The expected value of the income received from public assistance and social insurance programs is given by

$$E[Y_j] = p_j{}^*b_j \qquad (B.1)$$

where Y_j is the income received from program j, p_j is the probability that an individual receives income from program j, and b_j is the expected value of the benefits received by program j participants. The expected value of the annual benefit is estimated using the two-part model developed at RAND (Duan et al., 1983). This model is used to account for the large proportion of the population that receives no income from these programs. For each program, the probability of receiving public assistance in a year is estimated in the first step as a function of the individual's characteristics. In the second step, the annual income received from each program is estimated, conditional on income from the program being positive, again as a function of the individual's characteristics.

If the n observations are sorted so that the first N observations are on public assistance and the remaining n – N observations are not on public assistance, the likelihood function for the two-part model can be expressed as

$$L\left(\beta_1,\beta_2,\sigma^2_{\mu_2}\right)$$

$$= \left\{\prod_{i=1}^{N}\Phi\left(X_i\beta_1\right)\times\prod_{i=N+1}^{n}\left[1-\Phi\left(X_i\beta_1\right)\right]\right\}\times\left\{\prod_{i=1}^{N}\frac{1}{\sigma_{\mu_2}}\phi\left(\frac{Y_i-X_i\beta_2}{\sigma_{\mu_2}}\right)\right\} \quad \text{(B.2)}$$

where

Y	=	the annual income from a public assistance program
X	=	the set of explanatory variables, including educational attainment and demographic characteristics
Φ	=	the standard normal cumulative distribution function (c.d.f.)
ϕ	=	the standard normal probability distribution function (p.d.f.)
β_1 and β_2	=	parameters that relate program income to the explanatory variables
σ	=	the standard error (Duan et al., 1983)

This likelihood function can be separated into two components, each of which can be estimated separately. The first term,

$$\prod_{i=1}^{N} \Phi(X_i\beta_1) \times \prod_{i=N+1}^{n} \left[1 - \Phi(X_i\beta_1)\right]$$

is estimated using a probit; the second term,

$$\prod_{i=1}^{N} \frac{1}{\sigma_{\mu_2}} \phi\left(\frac{Y_i - X_i\beta_2}{\sigma_{\mu_2}}\right)$$

is estimated using ordinary least squares (OLS).

The probability of receiving public assistance from program j is estimated in the first part of the model using a probit. Whether or not an individual makes use of a public program is a dichotomous outcome: an individual either receives public aid during the year or does not. To model this outcome, the probit assumes that an unobserved variable, called Z, determines whether or not a positive outcome is observed. When Z exceeds a critical value, which we will refer to as Z^*, we observe that the individual uses the public program in question during the year; when Z is less than Z^*, we observe that the individual does not make use of the program. Z is normally distributed with a mean of zero and a standard deviation of one. The probability of program use can be estimated by evaluating the standard normal c.d.f. for the probit model's estimate of Z. The higher the value of Z, the greater the probability of program use. The unobserved variable Z is modeled by

$$Z_j = X\beta_1 + \mu_1, \quad \mu_1 \sim N(0,1) \tag{B.3}$$

X is a set of explanatory variables, including educational attainment, age, and demographic variables, and μ_1 is a random error term. The probability that an individual receives public assistance is given by

$$\Pr[Y_j > 0] = \Phi(Z_j) \tag{B.4}$$

where Φ is the standard normal c.d.f.

In the second part of the model, the income from public assistance program j of program participants (Y_j) is estimated with a linear model:

$$(Y_j | Z_j > Z_j^*) = X\beta_2 + \mu_2, \quad \mu_2 \sim N(0, \sigma^2 \mu_2) \tag{B.5}$$

The income from the public assistance programs is not distributed normally; therefore, the second part of the model is run on transformed data. The square root of income from welfare, food stamps and WIC, unemployment insurance, SSI, and Social Security was distributed approximately normally in the 1991 SIPP data. The natural log of the income from the school breakfast and lunch programs and low-income energy assistance was distributed approximately normally. Formally, income from welfare, food stamps and WIC, unemployment insurance, SSI, and Social Security is

$$(Y_j | Z_j > Z_j^*)^{1/2} = X\beta_2 + \mu_2, \quad \mu_2 \sim N(0, \sigma^2 \mu_2) \tag{B.6}$$

Income from the school lunch and breakfast programs and low-income energy assistance is

$$\ln(Y_j | Z_j > Z_j^*) = X\beta_2 + \mu_2, \quad \mu_2 \sim N(0, \sigma^2 \mu_2) \tag{B.7}$$

The maximum likelihood estimate for the two-part model is obtained by combining the estimate for β_1 in the first part of the model with the estimate for β_2 and $\sigma^2 \mu_2$ in the second part of the model. The expected value of income from welfare, food stamps and WIC, unemployment insurance, SSI, and Social Security is

$$E[Y_j] = P_j^* [(X\beta_2)^2 + \sigma^2 \mu_2] \tag{B.8}$$

where $P_j = \Pr[Y_j > 0] = \Phi(X\beta_1)$, and Φ is the standard normal c.d.f. The second part of the model produces unbiased consistent estimates of the square root of public assistance income. The square of the predicted values will not produce unbiased consistent estimates of public assistance income on the untransformed scale. σ^2 is added to the estimate of Y_{ij} to produce a consistent estimate on the untransformed scale.

The expected value of school breakfast and lunches and low-income energy assistance is

$$E[Y_j] = P_j^* \exp[(X\beta_2)^2 + \varphi] \qquad (B.9)$$

where

$$\varphi = \frac{1}{n} \sum_{i=1}^{n} e^{\ln y_i - X_i\beta_2}$$

φ is the smearing estimate used to produce consistent estimates of Y_j on the raw scale when the predicted values are retransformed from the log scale back (Duan et al., 1983). The smearing estimate is used rather than $\sigma^2/2$ because the residuals from the model of income from the school breakfast and lunch programs and the low-income energy assistance programs are not truly distributed log-normal.

Estimating the Value of Medicare and Medicaid Benefits

To estimate the value of the Medicare and Medicaid benefits received, we must compute the average cost per beneficiary of these programs. While the SIPP does not provide data on the value of the Medicare and Medicaid benefits received, it does provide data on whether each individual was hospitalized during the previous year. Because inpatient care is rarer and more expensive than outpatient care (Manning et al., 1987), these utilization data were used to calculate the cost of the benefits provided. We used these data in combination with the Medicare and Medicaid cost data described in Chapter Two to produce estimates of the expected value of Medicare and Medicaid benefits. If a Medicare or Medicaid beneficiary was hospitalized during the year, we used the average per-person program cost that includes the cost of hospitalization; if the beneficiary was not hospitalized during the year, we used the program cost for doctor visits and other outpatient care only. The SIPP population does not include residents of nursing homes, so the cost of long-term nursing facilities was not included in the average cost data; therefore, we may understate the value of the benefits received by the entire U.S. population.

Medicare and Medicaid benefits are modeled with an extension of the two-part model (Duan et al., 1983). The probability that an individual receives Medicare or Medicaid benefits during 1991 is estimated with a probit model:

$$Z^M_j = X\beta_3 + \mu_3, \quad \mu_3 \sim N(0,1) \tag{B.10}$$

for j = Medicare or Medicaid.

An individual receives Medicare or Medicaid when Z^M is greater than or equal to Z^{M*} and does not receive these benefits otherwise. If an individual receives either Medicare or Medicaid benefits during the year, the probability that he/she receives inpatient care during the year is estimated in a second step:

$$(Z^H_j | Z^M_j > = Z^{M*}_j) = X\beta_4 + \mu_4, \quad \mu_4 \sim N(0,1) \tag{B.11}$$

The average value of the Medicare and Medicaid benefits received is

$$E[Y_j] = \Phi(X\beta_3)*[C^A_j + \Phi(X\beta_4)*C^H_j] \tag{B.12}$$

where C^A_j is the average cost of ambulatory or outpatient care under Medicare or Medicaid, and C^H_j is the average cost of hospitalization under Medicare or Medicaid, as estimated in Chapter Two.

IMPLEMENTING THE TWO-PART MODEL

The two-part model was run separately for each of the public assistance and social insurance programs. The same basic model was run in each case: a probit model was used to estimate the probability of receiving public assistance during 1991, and OLS was used to estimate the 1991 program income of beneficiaries. The independent variables are

- Age and age-squared

- A set of dummy variables indicating the level of educational attainment: less than high school graduate (LTHSG), some college (SC), or a bachelor's degree or more (BDP); high school graduates are the reference group

- Interaction between the age and educational attainment variables

- A set of ethnicity indicators: black non-Hispanic, Asian, Mexican, and Other Hispanic; non-Hispanic whites are the reference group

- A dummy variable indicating whether the person is native-born or an immigrant

- A dummy variable indicating whether the person was a student during 1991

Consistent with human capital models of the effect of age and education on labor market outcomes, age is entered as a quadratic (Willis, 1986). This allows for the expected value of income from public programs to vary by age in a nonlinear fashion. Education was entered as a set of dummy variables to allow for a nonlinear effect of education on program income. The education variables were interacted with the age and age-squared terms to allow the effect of education on program income to vary by age. Therefore, the effect of education can diminish as a person moves away from his or her formal schooling. This also allows the effect of age to vary by educational attainment. While education may be measured with error, it is treated as an exogenous variable. Previous research indicates the potential bias introduced by excluding ability from the model is small (Ashenfelter and Krueger, 1992).

Separate models were run for men and women to be consistent with human capital models of labor market outcomes that allow for differences between men and women. (See, for example, Smith and Welch, 1986; Willis, 1986; Jaynes, 1990; Schoeni, McCarthy, and Vernez, 1996.) This allows for differences in the effect that education has on men's and women's program usage. We would expect differences in utilization of some programs that are directed toward women, such as AFDC and WIC. And the fact that women tend to earn less than men will affect the benefits they receive from programs such as Social Security and unemployment insurance, whose benefits are tied to earnings. In our discussion of the model in Chapter Two, we argue that income is one of the factors affecting program use; therefore, the differences in income between men and women should affect the demands they place on public assistance and social insurance programs, even if the benefits from these programs are not directly linked to earnings, income, or gender.

Dummy variables were entered for race and ethnicity and for immigrant status to allow the expected income from public programs to vary for each group. While it would have been preferable to estimate separate equations for each group, sample size restrictions made that impractical. For Social Security, SSI, Medicare, and Medicaid, separate models also were run for individuals under age 65 and those 65 or older, because these programs consist of separate components for the elderly and nonelderly.

The interpretation of the parameters from the model is complicated for several reasons. First, the coefficients from the probit model are not intuitive. They show the relationship between the independent variables and the underlying Z index. The probability that individual i participates in the program is given by the probability that Z_i is greater than the critical cutoff value, and is computed from the cumulative normal probability function. The effect of a change in an independent variable on the probability of program use depends on the initial probability of program use.

The second difficulty in interpreting the output of the model stems from its specification. Age is entered as a quadratic and is interacted with the educational attainment variables; therefore, the effect of education depends on the person's age. Also, the second part of the model is run on the square root of the income from most of the public assistance programs. Thus, the coefficients for the second part of the model are in terms of the square root of the program income.

The final difficulty in interpreting the model is due to the two-part model itself. The marginal effect of education on program benefits— the change in program income that reflects both the change in the participation rate and the change in the amount received by beneficiaries due to a change in education—is a combination of the parameters from the probit model and the OLS model and depends on the values of the independent variables. For welfare, food stamps and WIC, unemployment insurance, SSI, and Social Security, the marginal effect of a change in the X's is given by the first derivative of equation B.8:

$$\delta Y / \delta X = \beta_1 \phi(X\beta_1)*[(X\beta_2) + \sigma^2] + \Phi(X\beta_1)*[2\beta_2(X\beta_2)] \qquad (B.13)$$

where ϕ is the standard normal p.d.f. and Φ is the standard normal c.d.f. (The marginal effect for school breakfasts and lunches and low-income energy assistance is a similar term. Because the income from these programs is logged, the first derivative gives the percentage change in income for a change in X.) The marginal effect of education depends on the estimated education parameters and all the underlying explanatory variables; therefore, we evaluate the model for each program for a set of individuals with specific characteristics and show how the expected value changes with education. As an illustration, the analysis is described in detail for welfare programs (AFDC, General Assistance, and other welfare). The welfare model is an example of the two-part model that does not allow the return to education to vary between those under age 65 and those 65 and older. The SSI model, in contrast, models the effect of education on SSI separately for those under age 65 and those 65 and older. The models for Social Security, Medicare, and Medicaid also make this distinction.

The results of the two-part model for AFDC, General Assistance, and other welfare programs are shown in Table B.1 (standard errors are in parentheses). Most of the parameters in the probit model of welfare participation for men are not statistically significant, even at the 10 percent level. This reflects the relatively small number of adult men in households that receive welfare benefits. AFDC is primarily received by female-headed households, and General Relief is not available in all states. The individual education indicators are insignificant; taken as a whole, the education variables are not jointly significantly different from zero. The race variables are significant, indicating that minority men have a higher probability of welfare use. The age and age-squared variables are also significant; their signs indicate that expected benefits for the reference group increase at younger ages and then decrease. (The age and age-squared terms show the relation between age and the expected welfare benefit for high school graduates.)

The model provides a better explanation for the variance in welfare participation among women than among men. Minority women are

Table B.1

Parameter Estimates of Two-Part Model of 1991 Annual AFDC, General Assistance, and Other Welfare Income

Parameter	Probit Model		OLS Model	
	Men	Women	Men	Women
LTHSG	0.3379	0.3209	12.7967	20.5956*
	(0.3660)	(0.2274)	(16.4622)	(8.9146)
SC	-0.2046	-1.8676*	-25.2581	1.4156
	(0.4662)	(0.2786)	(24.2324)	(12.7085)
BDP	-0.7557	-2.8857*	-23.3132	-71.8201*
	(0.7835)	(0.6514)	(39.8936)	(41.0411)
Age	0.0346*	-0.0395*	1.1159	1.3791*
	(0.0150)	(0.0087)	(0.7275)	(0.3918)
Age^2	-0.0006*	0.0001	-0.0116	-0.0212*
	(0.0002)	(0.0001)	(0.0091)	(0.0049)
Age*LTHSG	-0.0048	0.0161	-0.6999	-0.9235*
	(0.0185)	(0.0116)	(0.8478)	(0.4791)
Age*SC	0.0099	0.0705*	1.4274	-0.2357
	(0.0247)	(0.0150)	(1.3417)	(0.6829)
Age*BDP	-0.0158	0.0737*	0.8556	2.4893
	(0.0355)	(0.0303)	(1.8203)	(1.8729)
Age^2*LTHSG	0.0001	-0.0002	0.0076	0.0103*
	(0.0002)	(0.0001)	(0.0103)	(0.0058)
Age^2*SC	0.0002	-0.0007*	-0.0187	0.0035
	(0.0003)	(0.0002)	(0.0173)	(0.0085)
Age^2*BDP	0.0004	-0.0005	-0.0075	-0.0205
	(0.0004)	(0.0003)	(0.0199)	(0.0201)
Black	0.3514*	0.7506*	2.5591	-0.2057
	(0.0561)	(0.0340)	(2.3924)	(1.2767)
Asian	0.5530*	0.3561*	18.8262*	11.5701*
	(0.1008)	(0.0794)	(4.2116)	(3.2068)
Mexican	0.1651*	0.1938*	-0.8905	5.3988*
	(0.7993)	(0.0561)	(3.2787)	(2.1580)
Other Hispanic	0.1590*	0.6499*	1.2728*	6.3468*
	(0.0960)	(0.0554)	(4.1191)	(1.9833)
Immigrant	0.0152	-0.0560	10.1759*	3.1901*
	(0.0698)	(0.0480)	(2.9782)	(1.8805)
Student	0.1025	0.1822*	6.1624	4.6084*
	(0.0647)	(0.0387)	(2.8315)	(1.4235)
Observations	26,769	31,361	465	1,637
σ	—	—	19.018	21.882

NOTE: Standard errors in parentheses. An asterisk indicates the variable is significant at the 10 percent level. LTHSG indicates less than a high school degree, HSG indicates a high school graduate, SC indicates some college, and BDP indicates at least a bachelor's degree.

more likely to be on welfare than are non-Hispanic whites, and immigrant women are less likely to use welfare than are native-borns (though the difference is not significant). The average benefit of welfare participants tends to be higher for immigrants than for natives. The participation rate of students in school during the sample is higher than that of nonstudents. The education parameters are jointly significantly different from zero and of the expected sign: welfare participation rates decline with educational attainment (though the participation rate of those with less than a high school diploma is not significantly different from that of high school graduates).

Because of the interaction between the education indicators and age and age-squared, the effect of education on welfare participation rates and the square root of welfare income is given by the coefficients on the education indicator variables plus the coefficients on the age and age-squared variables (the effect of education varies by age). Table B.2 summarizes the tests for whether the education and age interaction terms are jointly significantly different from zero. For the probit models, the test statistic is a chi-square. For the OLS models, the test statistic is an F-statistic. In each test, the null hypothesis is the education variable, and its interactions with age and age-squared are jointly equal to zero. The critical values and degrees of freedom for each test are shown in the bottom half of the table. (For the OLS models, the table shows degrees of freedom for the numerator and denominator, separated by a comma.)

Table B.2

Test of Joint Significance of Variables in Two-Part Model of Welfare Use

	Probit Model		OLS Model	
	Men	Women	Men	Women
Hypothesis to Be Tested	Test Statistic			
LTHSG, age*LTHSG, age^2*LTHSG = 0	57.28	300.04	0.43	3.27
SC, age*SC, age^2*SC = 0	27.81	133.04	0.42	0.65
BDP, age*BDP, age^2*BDP = 0	67.64	172.42	0.19	2.93
Degrees of Freedom and Critical Values				
Degrees of freedom	3	3	3, 447	3, 1619
Critical value	6.25	6.25	2.10	2.09

The probit model estimates the probability that an individual uses welfare during the year. The null hypothesis, that each education indicator and its interaction with age and age-squared is not jointly different from zero, can be rejected for both men and women in the probit model. This implies that the differences in participation rates by educational attainment are statistically significant, holding age constant.

The OLS model estimates the annual amount of welfare income received by welfare participants. The null hypothesis cannot be rejected in the OLS model for men. The interaction of the less-than-high-school-graduate (LTHSG) and the bachelor's-degree-plus (BDP) variables and their interaction with age and age-squared are each jointly significant in the OLS model for women. At each age, the benefits of women with high school diplomas are statistically different from those of women without a high school degree or who are college graduates.

The results of the two-part model for the other programs are shown in Tables B.3 through B.10. Table B.11 shows the model used to estimate the pretransfer after-tax income.

Table B.3

Parameter Estimates of Two-Part Model of Annual 1991 Supplemental Security Income

Parameter	Probit Model		OLS Model	
	Under 65	65+	Under 65	65+
		Men		
LTHSG	0.2763	-20.2655	-46.1039*	1176.0370
	(0.4827)	(23.7672)	(24.4345)	(1021.8760)
SC	-0.8182	-456.2476	-119.8063*	-18808.9400
	(0.6335)	(791.7864)	(37.7172)	(48450.1500)
BDP	0.3377	-516.4567	-69.3795	-9756.0340
	(1.1308)	(384.5482)	(67.7771)	(24749.5500)
Age	-0.0087	-0.9399	-0.7592	17.4308
	(0.0203)	(0.5890)	(1.0796)	(26.5791)
Age^2	0.0000	0.0063	0.0092	-0.1275
	(0.0003)	(0.0040)	(0.0135)	(0.1839)
Age*LTHSG	0.0080	0.5618	2.5417*	-33.0916
	(0.0259)	(0.6527)	(1.3011)	(28.3746)
Age*SC	0.0301	13.7336	6.4149*	568.0019
	(0.0348)	(23.7792)	(2.0607)	(1455.2760)
Age*BDP	-0.0438	14.8347	3.1785	268.6117
	(0.0594)	(11.1208)	(3.5874)	(717.5516)
Age^2*LTHSG	0.0000	-0.0038	-0.0314*	0.2312
	(0.0003)	(0.0045)	(0.0160)	(0.1959)
Age^2*SC	-0.0003	-0.1034	-0.0808*	-4.2863
	(0.0004)	(0.1785)	(0.0263)	(10.9248)
Age^2*BDP	0.0005	-0.1065	-0.0382	-1.8435
	(0.0007)	(0.0804)	(0.0445)	(5.1991)
Black	0.3947*	0.6827*	-5.5569*	-3.2690
	(0.0596)	(0.1180)	(2.7258)	(4.4430)
Asian	0.2975*	1.2963*	2.2161	13.9781
	(0.1419)	(0.2105)	(7.7875)	(7.1632)
Mexican	0.0349*	0.8901*	-7.9755*	2.8930*
	(0.0957)	(0.1725)	(4.4885)	(5.7482)
Other Hispanic	0.2663*	0.8375*	-0.8978	-2.8107
	(0.1026)	(0.1740)	(4.9228)	(6.4843)
Immigrant	-0.2174*	0.5237*	4.5206	12.8765*
	(0.0887)	(0.1236)	(4.7760)	(5.1205)
Student	0.0364	0.4112	-6.9241*	-8.6848
	(0.0758)	(0.4481)	(3.9577)	(16.2581)
Observations	23,093	3,676	375	143
σ	—	—	20.985	19.441

Table B.3 (continued)

Parameter	Probit Model		OLS Model	
	Under 65	65+	Under 65	65+
	Women			
LTHSG	0.2733	0.4104	-13.9912	427.1061
	(0.4179)	(13.3581)	(20.5231)	(515.9715)
SC	-0.7760	-10.4569	-32.7452	425.6902
	(0.5053)	(26.6601)	(27.6267)	(1394.7720)
BDP	0.1471	-30.7362	67.3175	2695.1980
	(1.1435)	(36.2138)	(87.6188)	(2005.0260)
Age	-0.0048	-0.2547	0.2563	14.9568
	(0.0150)	(0.3165)	(0.7751)	(13.1223)
Age^2	0.0001	0.0018	-0.0050	-0.0991
	(0.0002)	(0.0022)	(0.0091)	(0.0892)
Age*LTHSG	-0.0044	0.0009	0.8300	-11.3201
	(0.0213)	(0.3642)	(1.0206)	(14.1042)
Age*SC	0.0189	0.3129	1.4454	-10.7721
	(0.0263)	(0.7320)	(1.4062)	(38.1385)
Age*BDP	-0.0521	0.8187	-4.9508	-74.0933
	(0.0572)	(0.9809)	(4.2880)	(53.8446)
Age^2*LTHSG	0.0002	0.0000	-0.0101	0.0746
	(0.0003)	(0.0025)	(0.0118)	(0.0958)
Age^2*SC	-0.0001	-0.0024	-0.0153	0.0665
	(0.0003)	(0.0050)	(0.0168)	(0.2593)
Age^2*BDP	0.0007	-0.0055	0.0659	0.5076
	(0.0007)	(0.0066)	(0.0486)	(0.3600)
Black	0.5096*	0.9272*	0.4112	9.8365*
	(0.0457)	(0.0704)	(1.9825)	(2.0465)
Asian	0.1207	0.6982*	11.3208*	24.7740*
	(0.1159)	(0.1812)	(5.6855)	(5.6547)
Mexican	-0.0444	1.0493*	1.7117	8.1303*
	(0.0850)	(0.1291)	(3.8861)	(3.2833)
Other Hispanic	0.3631*	0.9058*	3.4267	15.9238*
	(0.0769)	(0.1245)	(3.3922)	(3.5578)
Immigrant	-0.0080	0.2608*	0.7558	6.7761*
	(0.0653)	(0.0876)	(3.0468)	(2.9078)
Student	-0.0100	0.2531	-6.2050*	-7.2240
	(0.0642)	(0.3332)	(3.2691)	(10.7804)
Observations	25,865	5,496	628	479
σ	—	—	21.064	18.512

NOTE: Standard errors in parentheses. An asterisk indicates the variable is significant at the 10 percent level. LTHSG indicates less than a high school graduate, HSG indicates a high school graduate, SC indicates some college, and BDP indicates at least a bachelor's degree.

Table B.4

Parameter Estimates of Two-Part Model of 1991 Annual Food Stamps and WIC Income

Parameter	Probit Model		OLS Model	
	Men	Women	Men	Women
LTHSG	0.4516*	0.2085	12.6124*	13.9218*
	(0.2371)	(0.1772)	(5.0510)	(4.1172)
SC	-0.9280*	-1.7542*	-14.5249	-20.5351*
	(0.3735)	(0.2155)	(10.3599)	(6.0645)
BDP	-1.1001*	-2.4148*	-30.6973*	-38.8120*
	(0.5536)	(0.4672)	(16.3580)	(19.3036)
Age	-0.0067	-0.0613*	0.7147*	0.3777*
	(0.0090)	(0.0062)	(0.2041)	(0.1664)
Age^2	-0.0001	0.0004*	-0.0085*	-0.0076*
	(0.0001)	(0.0001)	(0.0023)	(0.0019)
Age*LTHSG	-0.0005	0.0165*	-0.4473*	-0.5076*
	(0.0115)	(0.0083)	(0.2476)	(0.2062)
Age*SC	0.0370*	0.0641*	0.9116	0.9234*
	(0.0206)	(0.0111)	(0.6000)	(0.3173)
Age*BDP	0.0091	0.0512*	1.1509	1.3327
	(0.0255)	(0.0213)	(0.7683)	(0.8925)
Age^2*LTHSG	0.0000	-0.0001	0.0038	0.0048*
	(0.0001)	(0.0001)	(0.0027)	(0.0023)
Age^2*SC	-0.0005*	-0.0006*	-0.0137*	-0.0096*
	(0.0003)	(0.0001)	(0.0082)	(0.0038)
Age^2*BDP	0.0000	-0.0003	-0.0105	-0.0122
	(0.0003)	(0.0002)	(0.0085)	(0.0094)
Black	0.4750*	0.7965*	1.1223	5.3926*
	(0.0410)	(0.0286)	(0.8333)	(0.6368)
Asian	0.3543*	0.2008*	8.7626*	7.0147*
	(0.0879)	(0.0705)	(2.0329)	(1.8161)
Mexican	0.4137*	0.3889*	1.3352	-0.3022
	(0.0554)	(0.0451)	(1.0774)	(1.0085)
Other Hispanic	0.4606*	0.7012*	-1.7490	4.7662*
	(0.0642)	(0.0471)	(1.2913)	(1.0195)
Immigrant	-0.0458	-0.0438	0.3873	-2.0298*
	(0.0512)	(0.0393)	(1.0864)	(0.9301)
Student	-0.0787	0.0501	-1.4697	1.5864*
	(0.0511)	(0.0349)	(1.1332)	(0.7963)
Observations	26,769	31,361	1,233	2,981
σ	—	—	11.035	14.596

NOTE: Standard errors in parentheses. An asterisk indicates the variable is significant at the 10 percent level. LTHSG indicates less than a high school graduate, HSG indicates a high school graduate, SC indicates some college, and BDP indicates at least a bachelor's degree.

Table B.5

Parameter Estimates of Two-Part Model of 1991 Annual Low-Income Energy Assistance

Parameter	Probit Model		OLS Model	
	Men	Women	Men	Women
LTHSG	0.4629*	-0.1273	0.6459	0.0839
	(0.2554)	(0.1907)	(0.6470)	(0.4256)
SC	-0.3508	-1.3202*	-0.5465	-0.6442
	(0.3425)	(0.2246)	(0.9872)	(0.5953)
BDP	-1.0516*	-2.7120*	-1.7227	0.3468
	(0.5700)	(0.5189)	(1.8229)	(1.8552)
Age	-0.0109	-0.0477*	0.0155	-0.0050
	(0.0094)	(0.0062)	(0.0257)	(0.0155)
Age^2	0.0001	0.0005*	-0.0001	0.0001
	(0.0001)	(0.0001)	(0.0003)	(0.0002)
Age*LTHSG	-0.0026	0.0264*	-0.0289	-0.0027
	(0.0119)	(0.0086)	(0.0304)	(0.0196)
Age*SC	0.0061	0.0462*	0.0371	0.0354
	(0.0171)	(0.0107)	(0.0498)	(0.0284)
Age*BDP	0.014	0.0826*	0.0511	-0.0356
	(0.0252)	(0.0225)	(0.0777)	(0.0785)
Age^2*LTHSG	0.0000	-0.0003*	0.0003	0.0000
	(0.0001)	(0.0001)	(0.0003)	(0.0002)
Age^2*SC	-0.0001	-0.0004*	-0.0006	-0.0004
	(0.0002)	(0.0001)	(0.0006)	(0.0003)
Age^2*BDP	-0.0001	-0.0007*	-0.0004	0.0005
	(0.0003)	(0.0002)	(0.0008)	(0.0008)
Black	0.3749*	0.4758*	-0.3620*	-0.2381*
	(0.0443)	(0.0321)	(0.1006)	(0.0678)
Asian	0.1817*	-0.0796	-0.6450*	-0.3016
	(0.1099)	(0.0914)	(0.3107)	(0.2411)
Mexican	0.3215*	0.2483*	-1.1007*	-1.1226*
	(0.0623)	(0.0514)	(0.1341)	(0.1081)
Other Hispanic	0.2859*	0.4767*	-0.0055	0.1022
	(0.0751)	(0.0529)	(0.1719)	(0.1100)
Immigrant	-0.2342*	-0.1542*	0.0192	-0.1595
	(0.0604)	(0.0445)	(0.1539)	(0.1014)
Student	-0.1226*	0.1759*	-0.0136	0.2108*
	(0.0589)	(0.0393)	(0.1565)	(0.0883)
Observations	26,769	31,361	933	1,953
σ	—	—	1.1593	1.2006

NOTE: Standard errors in parentheses. An asterisk indicates the variable is significant at the 10 percent level. LTHSG indicates less than a high school graduate, HSG indicates a high school graduate, SC indicates some college, and BDP indicates at least a bachelor's degree.

Table B.6

Parameter Estimates of Two-Part Model of 1991 Annual Income from School Breakfast and Lunch Programs

	Probit Model		OLS Model	
Parameter	Men	Women	Men	Women
LTHSG	0.5838*	0.5967*	0.2852	0.5608
	(0.2190)	(0.1945)	(0.4300)	(-1.1084)
SC	-0.6642*	-1.3773*	-0.6386	-1.1084*
	(0.2607)	(0.2221)	(0.5723)	(0.4678)
BDP	-3.0742*	-3.2417*	-0.5092	-1.1307
	(0.4685)	(0.4375)	(1.2218)	(1.0656)
Age	0.0544*	0.0381*	0.0821*	0.0835*
	(0.0083)	(0.0070)	(0.0179)	(0.0139)
Age^2	-0.0009*	-0.0008*	-0.0010*	-0.0010*
	(0.0001)	(0.0001)	(0.0002)	(0.0002)
Age*LTHSG	-0.0177	-0.0119	-0.0088	-0.0104
	(0.0109)	(0.0095)	(0.0222)	(0.0185)
Age*SC	0.0160	0.0514*	0.0192	0.0490*
	(0.0139)	(0.0119)	(0.0318)	(0.0256)
Age*BDP	0.0995*	0.0991*	-0.0073	0.0218
	(0.0224)	(0.0212)	(0.0569)	(0.0496)
Age^2*LTHSG	0.0002*	0.0002	0.0002	0.0001
	(0.0001)	(0.0001)	(0.0003)	(0.0002)
Age^2*SC	-0.0001	-0.0008*	-0.0002	-0.0006*
	(0.0002)	(0.0002)	(0.0004)	(0.0003)
Age^2*BDP	-0.0009*	-0.0005*	0.0002	-0.0002
	(0.0003)	(0.0002)	(0.0007)	(0.0006)
Black	0.6554*	0.9074*	0.3575*	0.5065*
	(0.0330)	(0.0269)	(0.0608)	(0.0436)
Asian	0.4657*	0.3620*	0.2999*	0.1176
	(0.0627)	(0.0574)	(0.1177)	(0.1025)
Mexican	0.8264*	0.7381*	0.3814*	0.2749*
	(0.0435)	(0.0408)	(0.0732)	(0.0657)
Other Hispanic	0.4224*	0.6453*	0.2496*	0.4058*
	(0.0530)	(0.0443)	(0.0952)	(0.0716)
Immigrant	0.2120*	0.1569*	0.0099	-0.1035*
	(0.0387)	(0.0350)	(0.0681)	(0.0586)
Student	0.0651*	0.0222	0.1395*	0.1220*
	(0.0366)	(0.0303)	(0.0715)	(0.0586)
Observations	26,769	31,361	2,535	4,006
σ	—	—	1.087	1.1217

NOTE: Standard errors in parentheses. An asterisk indicates the variable is significant at the 10 percent level. LTHSG indicates less than a high school graduate, HSG indicates a high school graduate, SC indicates some college, and BDP indicates at least a bachelor's degree.

Table B.7

Parameter Estimates of Two-Part Model of 1991 Annual Unemployment Insurance

Parameter	Probit Model		OLS Model	
	Men	Women	Men	Women
LTHSG	-1.1053*	-0.9065*	-3.1831	-17.5634
	(0.2791)	(0.3049)	(12.3582)	(13.4960)
SC	-0.6367*	-0.6434*	-21.4946*	-18.2096
	(0.2692)	(0.2792)	(12.4180)	(12.8955)
BDP	-0.0068	-0.1228	0.7878	-2.4704
	(0.3690)	(0.4717)	(19.9351)	(26.5488)
Age	0.0487*	0.0508*	1.1806*	0.2576
	(0.0089)	(0.0086)	(0.4303)	(0.4026)
Age^2	-0.0008*	-0.0007*	-0.0125*	-0.0026
	(0.0001)	(0.0001)	(0.0056)	(0.0049)
Age*LTHSG	0.0577*	0.0509*	0.0665	0.7537
	(0.0143)	(0.0148)	(0.6642)	(0.6757)
Age*SC	0.0180	0.0209	1.3090*	1.1217*
	(0.0142)	(0.0142)	(0.6834)	(0.6740)
Age*BDP	-0.0247	-0.0059	-0.1767	0.2986
	(0.0184)	(0.0244)	(1.0533)	(1.4599)
Age^2*LTHSG	-0.0006*	-0.0006*	-0.0007	-0.0084
	(0.0002)	(0.0002)	(0.0083)	(0.0080)
Age^2*SC	-0.0001	-0.0002	-0.0175*	-0.0136
	(0.0002)	(0.0002)	(0.0089)	(0.0083)
Age^2*BDP	0.0003	-0.0000	0.0036	-0.0015
	(0.0002)	(0.0003)	(0.0132)	(0.0192)
Black	-0.0260	0.0103	-2.3149	-2.9165*
	(0.0415)	(0.0417)	(1.6434)	(1.6935)
Asian	-0.0798	-0.1368	-1.7506	-0.9274
	(0.0801)	(0.0871)	(3.4293)	(3.7104)
Mexican	0.1329*	0.1671*	-2.1264	0.4615
	(0.0528)	(0.0569)	(2.0628)	(2.2282)
Other Hispanic	-0.0518	-0.0168	-1.5778	2.5941
	(0.0657)	(0.0670)	(2.6730)	(2.6559)
Immigrant	-0.0213	0.0491	-0.8370	1.6257
	(0.0465)	(0.0484)	(1.9191)	(1.9518)
Student	-0.0411	0.1018*	1.5378	1.6226
	(0.0382)	(0.0387)	(1.5089)	(1.5146)
Observations	26,769	31,361	2,134	1,359
σ	—	—-	21.426	19.549

NOTE: Standard errors in parentheses. An asterisk indicates the variable is significant at the 10 percent level. LTHSG indicates less than a high school graduate, HSG indicates a high school graduate, SC indicates some college, and BDP indicates at least a bachelor's degree.

Table B.8

Parameter Estimates of Two-Part Model of 1991 Annual Social Security Income

Parameter	Probit Model		OLS Model	
	Under 65	65+	Under 65	65+
		Men		
LTHSG	-0.3525	-14.1550	23.2572	135.2562
	(0.3941)	(20.8862)	(19.1032)	(147.9074)
SC	-0.0815	-44.8509*	-15.8885	18.1418
	(0.4411)	(25.6483)	(24.9470)	(199.3800)
BDP	1.5833*	-38.6301	-86.5283*	-4.4746
	(0.7422)	(25.4961)	(50.1045)	(206.8789)
Age	-0.1984*	0.0864	2.8267*	8.4161*
	(0.0141)	(0.4473)	(0.6622)	(3.2403)
Age^2	0.0030*	-0.0002	-0.0230*	-0.0553*
	(0.0002)	(0.0031)	(0.0071)	(0.0222)
Age*LTHSG	0.0441*	0.4072	-0.9442	-3.5317
	(0.0202)	(0.5777)	(0.8823)	(4.0495)
Age*SC	-0.0042	1.2358*	1.0840	-0.3819
	(0.0232)	(0.7095)	(1.1961)	(5.4724)
Age*BDP	-0.1096*	1.0296	3.8879*	-0.0217
	(0.0358)	(0.7104)	(2.1393)	(5.6872)
Age^2*LTHSG	-0.0006*	-0.0029	0.0086	0.0223
	(0.0002)	(0.0040)	(0.0095)	(0.0276)
Age^2*SC	0.0000	-0.0085*	-0.0137	0.0022
	(0.0003)	(0.0049)	(0.0131)	(0.0374)
Age^2*BDP	0.0013*	-0.0068	-0.0409*	0.0020
	(0.0004)	(0.0049)	(0.0218)	(0.0389)
Black	0.2360*	-0.1615	-5.7817*	-6.7993*
	(0.0508)	(0.1407)	(1.7037)	(1.0794)
Asian	-0.2137	-0.9274*	-12.1817*	-9.2728*
	(0.1347)	(0.2031)	(4.8217)	(2.7248)
Mexican	-0.2176*	-0.2514	-8.5969*	-6.4594*
	(0.0886)	(0.2075)	(3.1803)	(1.9281)
Other Hispanic	-0.0009	-0.3264*	-5.3062	-6.1352*
	(0.0918)	(0.1880)	(3.2675)	(1.8197)
Immigrant	-0.2662*	-0.3697*	-2.8500	-1.5864
	(0.0718)	(0.1160)	(2.5493)	(1.0787)
Student	-0.1103	-0.2257	-2.7214	1.6211
	(0.0685)	(0.2824)	(3.0403)	(2.9535)
Observations	23,093	3,676	1,578	3,489
σ	—	—	21.572	17.051

Table B.8 (continued)

Parameter	Probit Model		OLS Model	
	Under 65	65+	Under 65	65+
		Women		
LTHSG	-0.5164	-4.6525	21.0184	54.4628
	(0.3721)	(15.3466)	(19.5888)	(107.6897)
SC	-1.3389*	-24.7205	-28.8890	-290.7727*
	(0.3823)	(21.4609)	(22.2633)	(148.3596)
BDP	-0.7264	-46.4898*	-10.3973	24.6335
	(0.6165)	(23.1123)	(44.9795)	(193.8350)
Age	-0.2270*	0.3316	1.5785*	8.2057*
	(0.0121)	(0.3410)	(0.6276)	(2.2053)
Age^2	0.0033*	-0.0022	-0.0154*	-0.0529*
	(0.0001)	(0.0023)	(0.0067)	(0.0150)
Age*LTHSG	0.0435*	0.1317	-1.1082	-1.5201
	(0.0189)	(0.4196)	(0.8870)	(2.9324)
Age*SC	0.0642*	0.6622	1.5065	7.9731*
	(0.0197)	(0.5883)	(1.0260)	(4.0479)
Age*BDP	0.0321	1.2254*	1.1012	-0.7362
	(0.0298)	(0.6334)	(1.9511)	(5.2776)
Age^2*LTHSG	-0.0005*	-0.0009	0.0119	0.0098
	(0.0002)	(0.0029)	(0.0094)	(0.0199)
Age^2*SC	-0.0007*	-0.0044	-0.0169	-0.0539*
	(0.0002)	(0.0040)	(0.0110)	(0.0275)
Age^2*BDP	-0.0004	-0.0081*	-0.0163	0.0059
	(0.0003)	(0.0043)	(0.0200)	(0.0358)
Black	0.1733*	-0.6894*	-6.8483*	-6.2010*
	(0.0442)	(0.0866)	(1.4868)	(0.8285)
Asian	-0.2959*	-0.9341*	-3.4474	-4.4424*
	(0.1157)	(0.1748)	(4.3191)	(2.2894)
Mexican	-0.0130	-0.4837*	-4.2572	-8.0399*
	(0.0740)	(0.1669)	(2.6523)	(1.6794)
Other Hispanic	0.0309	-0.6873*	-9.9237*	-5.2557*
	(0.0758)	(0.1395)	(2.6328)	(1.5915)
Immigrant	-0.2133*	-0.6065*	-2.9823	-1.6356*
	(0.0585)	(0.0933)	(2.0246)	(0.9093)
Student	-0.1335*	-0.2099	-0.6957	-0.4722
	(0.0569)	(0.3071)	(2.6438)	(2.8493)
Observations	25,865	5,496	2,079	5,234
σ	—	—	22.035	16.471

NOTE: Standard errors in parentheses. An asterisk indicates the variable is significant at the 10 percent level. LTHSG indicates less than a high school graduate, HSG indicates a high school graduate, SC indicates some college, and BDP indicates at least a bachelor's degree.

Table B.9

Parameter Estimates of Two-Part Model of 1991 Annual Medicare Income

Parameter	Medicare Use		Medicare Hospitalization	
	Under 65	65+	Under 65	65+
		Men		
LTHSG	0.1435	-13.1004	1.3263	-10.2114
	(0.4770)	(26.8567)	(1.8644)	(12.1643)
SC	0.3395	-11.5713	2.5184	-3.8015
	(0.5614)	(33.9819)	(2.3552)	(16.5541)
BDP	2.5747*	125.4347	1.5218	-35.1500*
	(0.7795)	(162.5590)	(4.9177)	(17.4018)
Age	-0.1364*	0.2040	0.1228*	-0.1131
	(0.0170)	(0.5257)	(0.0641)	(0.2664)
Age^2	0.0022*	-0.0013	-0.0014*	0.0010
	(0.0002)	(0.0036)	(0.0007)	(0.0018)
Age*LTHSG	0.0147	0.3379	-0.0551	0.2956
	(0.0236)	(0.7397)	(0.0814)	(0.3323)
Age*SC	-0.0279	0.3006	-0.1123	0.1130
	(0.0284)	(0.9374)	(0.1071)	(0.4536)
Age*BDP	-0.1486*	-3.8061	-0.1007	0.9959*
	(0.0376)	(4.7933)	(0.2053)	(0.4791)
Age^2*LTHSG	-0.0002	-0.0021	0.0005	-0.0021
	(0.0003)	(0.0051)	(0.0008)	(0.0023)
Age^2*SC	0.0004	-0.0019	0.0012	-0.0008
	(0.0003)	(0.0064)	(0.0011)	(0.0031)
Age^2*BDP	0.0017*	0.0288	0.0011	-0.0070*
	(0.0004)	(0.0353)	(0.0020)	(0.0033)
Black	0.3327*	-0.1709	-0.2080	0.0273
	(0.0549)	(0.1923)	(0.1382)	(0.0871)
Asian	-0.2296	-1.0802*	-0.2840	-0.4369
	(0.1585)	(0.2236)	(0.4595)	(0.2699)
Mexican	-0.1381	0.0617	-0.0571	0.3137*
	(0.0985)	(0.3135)	(0.2589)	(0.1456)
Other Hispanic	-0.0087	-0.1520	-0.0022	0.0655
	(0.1067)	(0.2581)	(0.2704)	(0.1481)
Immigrant	-0.2196*	-0.5355*	0.1241	-0.1805*
	(0.0808)	(0.1470)	(0.2086)	(0.0918)
Student	-0.2220*	-0.0149	-0.0808	-0.3596
	(0.0876)	(0.4605)	(0.2978)	(0.2769)
Observations	23,518	3,750	990	3,680

Table B.9 (continued)

Parameter	Medicare Use		Medicare Hospitalization	
	Under 65	65+	Under 65	65+
	Women			
LTHSG	-0.6294	-13.5725	2.2968	7.1194
	(0.4693)	(22.1743)	(2.1507)	(9.4624)
SC	-0.4231	37.0164	0.7868	8.5832
	(0.5233)	(34.8556)	(2.5291)	(13.3792)
BDP	0.2207	-57.4913*	3.6493	-35.8376*
	(0.7396)	(33.3100)	(4.0123)	(17.4296)
Age	-0.2155*	0.2510	0.1301*	-0.1040
	(0.0157)	(0.4853)	(0.0749)	(0.1960)
Age^2	0.0031*	-0.0016	-0.0014*	0.0009
	(0.0002)	(0.0033)	(0.0008)	(0.0013)
Age*LTHSG	0.0524*	0.3731	-0.0784	-0.1888
	(0.0235)	(0.6084)	(0.0937)	(0.2572)
Age*SC	0.0060	-1.0256	0.0022	-0.2274
	(0.0273)	(0.9646)	(0.1125)	(0.3644)
Age*BDP	-0.0085	1.5595*	-0.1518	0.9670*
	(0.0364)	(0.9138)	(0.1759)	(0.4727)
Age^2*LTHSG	-0.0006*	-0.0025	0.0007	0.0013
	(0.0003)	(0.0042)	(0.0010)	(0.0017)
Age^2*SC	0.0000	0.0071	-0.0003	0.0015
	(0.0003)	(0.0067)	(0.0012)	(0.0025)
Age^2*BDP	0.0000	-0.0106*	0.0015	-0.0065*
	(0.0004)	(0.0062)	(0.0018)	(0.0032)
Black	0.0842	-0.6325*	-0.1032	0.0096
	(0.0563)	(0.1234)	(0.1440)	(0.0709)
Asian	-0.2963*	-0.9737*	-0.1328	-0.4755*
	(0.1516)	(0.2061)	(0.4391)	(0.2353)
Mexican	-0.1326	-0.3207	-0.0401	-0.0086
	(0.0984)	(0.2397)	(0.2557)	(0.1435)
Other Hispanic	0.1343	-0.3238	-0.0910	0.0750
	(0.0897)	(0.2117)	(0.2238)	(0.1300)
Immigrant	-0.2133*	-0.6588*	-0.0538	-0.0256
	(0.0742)	(0.1299)	(0.1916)	(0.0784)
Student	-0.1762*	-0.1810	-0.2980	-0.1969
	(0.0804)	(0.4338)	(0.2865)	(0.2820)
Observations	26,267	5,606	1,047	5,516

NOTE: Standard errors in parentheses. An asterisk indicates the variable is significant at the 10 percent level. LTHSG indicates less than a high school graduate, HSG indicates a high school graduate, SC indicates some college, and BDP indicates at least a bachelor's degree.

Table B.10

Parameter Estimates of Two-Part Model of 1991 Annual Medicaid Income

Parameter	Medicaid Use		Medicaid Hospitalization	
	Under 65	65+	Under 65	65+
	Men			
LTHSG	0.2572	-9.4988	1.0265	3.5541
	(0.3507)	(18.5466)	(1.1256)	(52.8389)
SC	-0.7378*	-51.9254	2.5562	-407.0021
	(0.4313)	(37.6455)	(1.6147)	(1338.298)
BDP	0.1744	-53.6641	-9.8291	-132.2925
	(0.7408)	(46.5767)	(7.3014)	(207.8664)
Age	0.0033	-0.7915*	0.0267	0.2757
	(0.0143)	(0.4423)	(0.0486)	(1.3032)
Age^2	-0.0002	0.0054*	0.0000	-0.0012
	(0.0002)	(0.0030)	(0.0006)	(0.0088)
Age*LTHSG	0.0061	0.2713	-0.0368	-0.0095
	(0.0190)	(0.5071)	(0.0596)	(1.4328)
Age*SC	0.0175	1.4430	-0.1156	12.5796
	(0.0240)	(1.0417)	(0.0875)	(39.8354)
Age*BDP	-0.0572	1.5125	0.4524	3.8497
	(0.0377)	(1.3035)	(0.3249)	(5.9483)
Age^2*LTHSG	0.0000	-0.0018	0.0002	-0.0006
	(0.0002)	(0.0034)	(0.0007)	(0.0097)
Age^2*SC	-0.0001	-0.0100	0.0012	-0.0969
	(0.0003)	(0.0072)	(0.0011)	(0.2964)
Age^2*BDP	0.0009*	-0.0107	-0.0051	-0.0278
	(0.0005)	(0.0091)	(0.0035)	(0.0425)
Black	0.4160*	0.6242*	-0.2613*	0.1802
	(0.0453)	(0.1030)	(0.1329)	(0.2440)
Asian	0.4401*	1.0836*	-0.9971*	-0.9999*
	(0.0906)	(0.1947)	(0.4699)	(0.5972)
Mexican	0.0777	0.7898*	-0.1410	0.5443*
	(0.0668)	(0.1579)	(0.1964)	(0.3261)
Other Hispanic	0.2761*	0.8592*	-0.1567	-0.0551
	(0.0739)	(0.1520)	(0.2152)	(0.3446)
Immigrant	-0.0328	0.4755*	-0.2012	-0.2527
	(0.0583)	(0.1062)	(0.1875)	(0.2783)
Student	0.0878*	0.4970	-0.4572*	0.2796
	(0.0522)	(0.3391)	(0.2045)	(0.9196)
Observations	23,518	3,750	940	219

Table B.10 (continued)

Parameter	Medicaid Use		Medicaid Hospitalization	
	Under 65	65+	Under 65	65+
	Women			
LTHSG	0.6172*	-3.1554	-0.0061	-19.1630
	(0.2552)	(11.9174)	(0.5441)	(30.2888)
SC	-1.8910*	-1.7355	-0.5506	62.2851
	(0.2777)	(21.3388)	(0.7668)	(72.8252)
BDP	-2.3510*	-22.7643	0.2423	-17496.130
	(0.6604)	(31.9436)	(2.6563)	(5458505)
Age	-0.0655*	-0.1280	-0.1128*	-0.4072
	(0.0094)	(0.2789)	(0.0238)	(0.7516)
Age^2	0.0005*	0.0009	0.0013*	0.0028
	(0.0001)	(0.0019)	(0.0003)	(0.0051)
Age*LTHSG	-0.0031	0.0962	0.0050	0.5159
	(0.0138)	(0.3250)	(0.0310)	(0.8272)
Age*SC	0.0715*	0.0341	0.0402	-1.7409
	(0.0157)	(0.5814)	(0.0444)	(1.9831)
Age*BDP	0.0455	0.6043	0.0178	446.1840
	(0.0335)	(0.8678)	(0.1357)	(139116.8)
Age^2*LTHSG	0.0001	-0.0006	-0.0001	-0.0035
	(0.0002)	(0.0022)	(0.0004)	(0.0056)
Age^2*SC	-0.0007*	-0.0002	-0.0006	0.0121
	(0.0002)	(0.0039)	(0.0006)	(0.0134)
Age^2*BDP	-0.0002	-0.0041	-0.0006	-2.8426
	(0.0004)	(0.0059)	(0.0016)	(885.7281)
Black	0.7247*	0.9290*	-0.3545*	-0.2402*
	(0.0308)	(0.0661)	(0.0708)	(0.1344)
Asian	0.2152*	0.9324*	-0.2409	-0.9369*
	(0.0719)	(0.1646)	(0.1847)	(0.4990)
Mexican	0.2479*	0.9706*	0.1140	-0.2090
	(0.0478)	(0.1249)	(0.1019)	(0.2359)
Other Hispanic	0.6376*	0.9971*	-0.1329	0.1078
	(0.0494)	(0.1187)	(0.1041)	(0.2317)
Immigrant	-0.0135	0.2211*	0.0691	-0.1283
	(0.0414)	(0.0819)	(0.0951)	(0.1946)
Student	0.0993*	0.0629	-0.3710*	0.2747
	(0.0347)	(0.3349)	(0.0833)	(0.7560)
Observations	26,267	5,606	2,677	654

NOTE: Standard errors in parentheses. An asterisk indicates the variable is significant at the 10 percent level. LTHSG indicates less than a high school graduate, HSG indicates a high school graduate, SC indicates some college, and BDP indicates at least a bachelor's degree.

Table B.11

Parameter Estimates of OLS Model of 1991 Annual Pretransfer After-Tax Income

Parameter	OLS Model	
	Men	Women
LTHSG	0.1403*	0.2337*
	0.0743	0.0725
SC	0.3564*	0.2158*
	0.0707	0.0634
BDP	0.1141	0.2802*
	0.0876	0.0848
Age	0.0362*	0.0471*
	0.0022	0.0019
Age^2	-0.0003*	-0.0005*
	0.0000	0.0000
Age*LTHSG	-0.0166*	-0.0241*
	0.0034	0.0031
Age*SC	-0.0083*	-0.0006
	0.0034	0.0029
Age*BDP	0.0145*	0.0078*
	0.0040	0.0038
Age^2*LTHSG	0.0002*	0.0002*
	0.0000	0.0000
Age^2*SC	0.0001*	0.0000
	0.0000	0.0000
Age^2*BDP	-0.0001*	-0.0001*
	0.0000	0.0000
Black	0.0111*	-0.3055*
	0.0132	0.0117
Asian	-0.0841*	0.0064
	0.0238	0.0226
Mexican	-0.2388*	-0.2657*
	0.0183	0.0180
Other Hispanic	-0.0682*	-0.2403*
	0.0208	0.0195
Immigrant	-0.2719*	-0.0549*
	0.0142	0.0135
Student	-0.2366	-0.0592*
	0.0123	0.0113
Observations	26,270	30,064
σ	0.5824	0.5959

NOTE: Standard errors in parentheses. An asterisk indicates the variable is significant at the 10 percent level. LTHSG indicates less than a high school graduate, HSG indicates a high school graduate, SC indicates some college, and BDP indicates at least a bachelor's degree.

THE ELDERLY: A SPECIAL CASE

Education's effect on social insurance programs for the elderly, such as Social Security and Medicare, differs from its effect on the other public programs discussed in Chapter Two. Unlike those other programs, social insurance programs base eligibility on the level and length of contributions made during the working lives of the elderly. Elderlies who are ineligible for Social Security or Medicare benefits or whose benefits are insufficient may be eligible to receive Supplemental Security Income for the Aged (SSI-A) and Medicaid. Because many immigrants have had no attachment to the labor force in the United States, they are more likely to fall into this latter category than are native-borns (McCarthy and Vernez, 1997; Vernez, 1999).

Table C.1 displays the average annual spending per woman age 75 in Social Security and SSI-A.[1] It shows that average spending on Social Security increases slightly with educational attainment, reflecting the higher contributions made by those with higher levels of education. There are only marginal variations in average Social Security benefits across ethnic groups, with one notable exception. The average Social Security benefits of non-Hispanic white women are about 20 percent higher than those of other women at every level of education. This reflects, in part, the higher incomes of non-Hispanic whites.

The average Social Security benefits of elderly immigrant women are from 10 to 20 percent lower than the benefits received by elderly native-born women. This is primarily because immigrants are less likely to be eligible to receive Social Security than are native-borns,

_____

[1]The spending levels and patterns for men are similar and hence are not shown.

and when they are eligible, they receive lower benefits. Many elderly immigrants come here to reunite with family members and have not worked in the United States. Others with low levels of education may have contributed minimally to Social Security and hence receive the lower scale benefits.

The net result of this pattern is captured in the bottom half of Table C.1, which compares SSI spending for immigrant and native-born women age 75. It shows that the average SSI benefit is typically twice as large for immigrants as for native-borns, regardless of level of education and regardless of ethnic group. However, since SSI is a means-tested program, the amount of the SSI benefits declines sharply with educational attainment—the opposite of what happens with Social Security benefits, where the amount increases with educational attainment.

Table C.1

Average Annual Social Security and SSI Spending per Woman Age 75, by Educational Attainment, Ethnicity, and Nativity (1997 dollars)

Educational Attainment	Asian		Black		Mexican		Other Hispanic		Non-Hispanic White	
	N	I	N	I	N	I	N	I	N	I
Social Security										
High school dropout	5,833	4,486	5,863	4,771	5,757	4,873	6,013	4,901	7,347	6,674
High school graduate	6,637	5,242	6,641	5,525	6,507	5,613	6,802	5,668	8,166	7,501
Some college	7,337	5,854	7,338	6,159	7,194	6,253	7,509	6,312	8,936	8,247
College graduate	6,814	5,211	6,890	5,585	6,801	5,742	7,054	5,726	8,570	7,980
Supplemental Security Income for the Aged										
High school dropout	1,299	2,128	1,064	1,741	1,139	1,918	1,273	2,054	187	385
High school graduate	555	1,021	513	938	582	1,044	604	1,089	57	135
Some college	240	485	225	450	260	513	269	531	18	48
College graduate	321	626	295	573	338	647	352	676	27	69

NOTE: N = native-born; I = immigrant.

This pattern of benefits to the elderly in Social Security and its complementary SSI-A program is replicated for the elderly in Medicare and its complement, the Medicaid program, with one exception. Average Medicare spending per elderly person remains relatively constant as educational attainment increases. It is, however, higher for college graduates. There are also no major variations in Medicare spending across ethnic groups, with the exception of Asians. Average Medicare spending is generally 30 percent lower per Asian elderly person than per elderly in any other ethnic group.

SAVINGS IN PROGRAM EXPENDITURES AND INCREASES IN TAX REVENUES AND DISPOSABLE INCOME ASSOCIATED WITH INCREASED EDUCATIONAL ATTAINMENT

The four tables in this appendix show our estimates of the savings in program expenditures, the increases in tax revenues, and the increases in disposable income associated with increases in education for native-born and immigrant women and men age 30. Values are in 1997 dollars for three discrete increases in level of education—from high school dropout to high school graduate, from high school graduate to some college, and from some college to college graduate—and for each ethnicity. These tables contain the values used for Figures 2.4, 2.5, and 2.6 in Chapter Two.

Table D.1

Savings in Public Social Programs and Increases in Tax Revenues and Disposable Income Associated with Discrete Increases in Educational Attainment for Native-Born Women Age 30 (1997 dollars)

	Asian	Black	Mexican	Other Hispanic	Non-Hispanic White
High School Dropout to High School Graduate					
Program savings	2556	2841	2438	3080	1409
Tax revenues	2378	1819	1843	1951	2295
Disposable income	3397	2487	2588	2655	3376
High School Graduate to Some College					
Program savings	682	1101	1956	1348	431
Tax revenues	1834	1339	1398	1428	2691
Disposable income	3152	2307	2401	2463	3132
Some College to College Graduate					
Program savings	625	1065	411	843	278
Tax revenues	3310	2463	2551	2613	3138
Disposal income	4885	3577	3722	3817	4854

Table D.2

Savings in Public Social Programs and Increases in Tax Revenues and Disposable Income Associated with Discrete Increases in Educational Attainment for Immigrant Women Age 30 (1997 dollars)

	Asian	Black	Mexican	Other Hispanic	Non-Hispanic White
High School Dropout to High School Graduate					
Program savings	1974	2299	2419	3318	1272
Tax revenues	2378	1770	1785	1896	2226
Disposable income	3216	2354	2450	2513	3195
High School Graduate to Some College					
Program savings	669	949	1097	1419	423
Tax revenues	1781	1299	1358	1388	1709
Disposable income	2983	2184	2273	2331	2964
Some College to College Graduate					
Program savings	552	1036	359	761	272
Tax revenues	3166	2400	2142	2545	3056
Disposal income	4624	3385	3523	3613	4595

Table D.3

Savings in Public Social Programs and Increases in Tax Revenues and Disposable Income Associated with Discrete Increases in Educational Attainment for Native-Born Men Age 30 (1997 Dollars)

	Asian	Black	Mexican	Other Hispanic	Non-Hispanic White
High School Dropout to High School Graduate					
Program savings	3963	7064	3849	3692	2037
Tax revenues	1860	1039	1522	1736	1930
Disposable income	2677	2257	2184	2262	2866
High School Graduate to Some College					
Program savings	456	1083	583	792	378
Tax revenues	1402	1157	1134	1174	1465
Disposable income	2714	2289	2214	2294	2906
Some College to College Graduate					
Program savings	484	987	514	590	335
Tax revenues	3074	2660	2577	2676	3193
Disposal income	4489	3784	3661	3793	4805

Table D.4

Savings in Public Social Programs and Increases in Tax Revenues and Disposable Income Associated with Discrete Increases in Educational Attainment for Immigrant Men Age 30 (1997 dollars)

	Asian	Black	Mexican	Other Hispanic	Non-Hispanic White
High School Dropout to High School Graduate					
Program savings	802	2806	910	1269	1186
Tax revenues	1724	1516	1416	1501	1791
Disposable income	2461	2075	2008	2080	2635
High School Graduate to Some College					
Program savings	612	743	187	822	175
Tax revenues	1314	1086	1066	1103	1372
Disposable income	2496	2104	2036	2109	2672
Some College to College Graduate					
Program savings	369	—	217	341	274
Tax revenues	2900	2516	2445	2523	3018
Disposal income	4127	3479	3366	3487	4418

EDUCATION FLOW RATES

The RAND Education Simulation Model requires annual flow rates into and out of the postelementary school system by person age and by population group. At first thought, the estimation of these rates would seem to be straightforward. For example, to find out what happens to students in 9th grade from one year to the next, count the number of 9th graders at the start of a school year; then, a year later, count how many are (a) still in 9th grade, (b) in 10th grade, and (c) out of high school. Dividing the latter three counts by the first gives the annual flow rates for 9th graders.

However, as usual, data limitations make parameter estimation complex. The Current Population Survey (CPS), starting in 1992, asks education status for both the current year and the previous year, so we can estimate annual flow rates at the national level. (The 1990 Census did not ask this dual question.) However, the CPS sample does not permit analysis of location (California vs. the rest of the nation), and the CPS (in the survey month that asks the dual education-status question) did not ask nativity (native-born vs. immigrant).

To get around these limitations, we constructed flow rates for aggregate population groups defined by ethnicity and gender and then used the 1990 Census to add the location and nativity distinctions. We added those distinctions by tuning the flow rates until the projected educational attainment of a cohort agreed with the educational attainment observed by the 1990 Census. There still remained a problem, however: We could do this tuning only for native-borns, because the educational attainment of immigrant populations is in large part a result of the education they receive in their country of origin before immigrating to the United States. Our information on the educational attainment of arriving immigrants is from the 1990 Census. It is not reasonable to assume that the educational attainment of immigrants who arrived during the decades before 1990 (and who were 40 years old in 1990) is equal to that of immigrants who arrived in 1990. So, we could not tune the education flow rates for immigrants to hit 1990 attainment targets for 40-year-olds. Hence, we used the tuned flow rates for native-born people of the same ethnicity, gender, and location.

As a result of the above considerations, the required annual flow rates into and out of the postelementary school system were estimated in five steps:

1. Estimate national average flow rates for population groups defined by ethnicity and gender using the CPS for 1992–1994.

2. Estimate national average flow rates by person age using the 1992–1994 CPS.

3. Use the ratio of the average rate for a population group to the national average rate (step 1) to adjust the national averages by person age (step 2) into estimates of flow rates by person age for the population groups defined by ethnicity and gender.

4. Adjust the national flow rates by person age and population group (step 3) until the projected educational attainment of 40-year-old native-borns in California agrees with that observed in the 1990 Census. Do the same for the rest of the nation.

5. Use the flow rates estimated for native-borns (by ethnicity, age, gender, and location) for immigrants (by ethnicity, age, gender, and location).

Tables E.1 through E.4 illustrate the resulting annual flow rates into and out of education in California by grade and age for two of our 20 population groups: native-born non-Hispanic white males and native-born Mexican males.

Tables E.1 and E.2 display the annual flow rates from 9th to 10th grade and so on to graduate school or out of school. For each of the first three high school grades, the tables display the probability that a member of the population group will stay in that grade, advance to the next grade, or "exit to some HS" (i.e., join the group described as having some high school). For those in 12th grade, the tables show the probability that a member of the population group will repeat that grade, "exit to HSD" (i.e., get a high school degree), advance to college, or exit to some HS. For instance, Tables E.1 and E.2 show that 4.8 percent of native-born Mexican males age 17 in the 12th grade will repeat the grade and 41.4 percent will advance to college, compared to 2.1 percent and 53.0 percent, respectively, for their non-Hispanic white counterparts. For the first year of college, the two tables show the probability that an individual will remain in the same year of college, will advance to the next year, or will "exit to some college" (i.e., exit with no degree). For the other college years shown, these probabilities are joined by the probabilities that an individual will "exit to AD" (i.e., exit with an associate degree), "exit to BD" (with a bachelor's degree), or "exit to GD" (with a graduate degree), as appropriate.

Tables E.3 and E.4 display, for the same two population groups, the annual flow rates of those "not in school" back to school by level of education and age. For instance, Tables E.3 and E.4 show that a 20-year-old native-born Mexican male with no high school degree has a 5.7 percent probability of returning to school, whereas his non-Hispanic white counterpart has a 6.3 percent probability of doing so.

Table E.1

Annual Flow Rates Within and Out of Schools for Native-Born Mexican Males in California, by Age and Grade

a. From 9th, 10th, and 11th Grade

Age	From 9th Grade			From 10th Grade			From 11th Grade		
	Stay in 9th	Advance to 10th	Exit to Some HS	Stay in 10th	Advance to 11th	Exit to Some HS	Stay in 11th	Advance to 12th	Exit to Some HS
12	0.000	1.000	0.000	0.097	0.903	0.000	0.021	0.979	0.000
13	0.000	1.000	0.000	0.097	0.903	0.000	0.021	0.979	0.000
14	0.014	0.986	0.000	0.097	0.903	0.000	0.021	0.979	0.000
15	0.037	0.963	0.000	0.039	0.961	0.000	0.021	0.979	0.000
16	0.050	0.882	0.069	0.055	0.945	0.000	0.005	0.995	0.000
17	0.072	0.727	0.201	0.083	0.811	0.106	0.010	0.950	0.040
18	0.072	0.727	0.201	0.083	0.710	0.207	0.017	0.816	0.167
19	0.072	0.727	0.201	0.083	0.710	0.207	0.032	0.582	0.386
20	0.072	0.727	0.201	0.083	0.710	0.207	0.032	0.582	0.386
21	0.072	0.727	0.201	0.083	0.710	0.207	0.032	0.582	0.386
22	0.072	0.727	0.201	0.083	0.710	0.207	0.032	0.582	0.386
23	0.072	0.727	0.201	0.083	0.710	0.207	0.032	0.582	0.386
24	0.072	0.727	0.201	0.083	0.710	0.207	0.032	0.582	0.386
25	0.072	0.727	0.201	0.083	0.710	0.207	0.032	0.582	0.386
26	0.072	0.727	0.201	0.083	0.710	0.207	0.032	0.582	0.386
27	0.072	0.727	0.201	0.083	0.710	0.207	0.032	0.582	0.386
28	0.072	0.727	0.201	0.083	0.710	0.207	0.032	0.582	0.386
29	0.072	0.727	0.201	0.083	0.710	0.207	0.032	0.582	0.386
30	0.072	0.727	0.201	0.083	0.710	0.207	0.032	0.582	0.386
31	0.072	0.727	0.201	0.083	0.710	0.207	0.032	0.582	0.386
32	0.072	0.727	0.201	0.083	0.710	0.207	0.032	0.582	0.386
33	0.072	0.727	0.201	0.083	0.710	0.207	0.032	0.582	0.386
34	0.072	0.727	0.201	0.083	0.710	0.207	0.032	0.582	0.386
35	0.072	0.727	0.201	0.083	0.710	0.207	0.032	0.582	0.386
36	0.072	0.727	0.201	0.083	0.710	0.207	0.032	0.582	0.386
37	0.072	0.727	0.201	0.083	0.710	0.207	0.032	0.582	0.386
38	0.072	0.727	0.201	0.083	0.710	0.207	0.032	0.582	0.386
39	0.000	0.000	1.000	0.000	0.000	1.000	0.000	0.000	1.000

Table E.1 (continued)

b. From 12th Grade, College Year 1

Age	From 12th Grade					From College Year 1		
	Stay in 12th	Advance to College	Exit to Some HS	Exit to 12th ND	Exit to HSD	Stay in C1	Advance to C2	Exit to Some Col
12	0.131	0.434	0.095	0.008	0.332	0.183	0.561	0.256
13	0.131	0.434	0.095	0.008	0.332	0.183	0.561	0.256
14	0.131	0.434	0.095	0.008	0.332	0.183	0.561	0.256
15	0.131	0.434	0.095	0.008	0.332	0.183	0.561	0.256
16	0.131	0.434	0.095	0.008	0.332	0.183	0.561	0.256
17	0.048	0.414	0.111	0.022	0.405	0.183	0.561	0.256
18	0.098	0.301	0.022	0.029	0.550	0.116	0.611	0.273
19	0.185	0.201	0.000	0.067	0.548	0.140	0.533	0.327
20	0.125	0.091	0.000	0.088	0.696	0.201	0.460	0.339
21	0.125	0.091	0.000	0.088	0.696	0.182	0.455	0.363
22	0.125	0.091	0.000	0.088	0.696	0.248	0.433	0.319
23	0.125	0.091	0.000	0.088	0.696	0.203	0.433	0.364
24	0.125	0.091	0.000	0.088	0.696	0.249	0.390	0.361
25	0.125	0.091	0.000	0.088	0.696	0.292	0.301	0.408
26	0.125	0.091	0.000	0.088	0.696	0.290	0.273	0.436
27	0.125	0.091	0.000	0.088	0.696	0.235	0.341	0.424
28	0.125	0.091	0.000	0.088	0.696	0.268	0.379	0.354
29	0.125	0.091	0.000	0.088	0.696	0.271	0.323	0.405
30	0.125	0.091	0.000	0.088	0.696	0.271	0.323	0.405
31	0.125	0.091	0.000	0.088	0.696	0.271	0.323	0.405
32	0.125	0.091	0.000	0.088	0.696	0.271	0.323	0.405
33	0.125	0.091	0.000	0.088	0.696	0.271	0.323	0.405
34	0.125	0.091	0.000	0.088	0.696	0.271	0.323	0.405
35	0.125	0.091	0.000	0.088	0.696	0.271	0.323	0.405
36	0.125	0.091	0.000	0.088	0.696	0.271	0.323	0.405
37	0.125	0.091	0.000	0.088	0.696	0.271	0.323	0.405
38	0.125	0.091	0.000	0.088	0.696	0.271	0.323	0.405
39	0.000	0.000	1.000	0.000	0.000	0.000	0.000	1.000

Table E.1 (continued)

c. From College Year 2, College Year 3

	From College Year 2				From College Year 3			
Age	Stay in C2	Advance to C3	Exit to Some Col	Exit to AD	Stay in C3	Advance to C4	Exit to Some Col	Exit to AD
12	0.167	0.595	0.217	0.021	0.169	0.354	0.397	0.080
13	0.167	0.595	0.217	0.021	0.169	0.354	0.397	0.080
14	0.167	0.595	0.217	0.021	0.169	0.354	0.397	0.080
15	0.167	0.595	0.217	0.021	0.169	0.354	0.397	0.080
16	0.167	0.595	0.217	0.021	0.169	0.354	0.397	0.080
17	0.167	0.595	0.217	0.021	0.169	0.354	0.397	0.080
18	0.167	0.595	0.217	0.021	0.169	0.354	0.397	0.080
19	0.117	0.615	0.248	0.020	0.169	0.354	0.397	0.080
20	0.120	0.569	0.267	0.044	0.059	0.413	0.503	0.026
21	0.137	0.524	0.302	0.037	0.083	0.363	0.515	0.040
22	0.169	0.428	0.350	0.053	0.116	0.337	0.487	0.059
23	0.186	0.433	0.306	0.075	0.120	0.315	0.463	0.102
24	0.162	0.432	0.319	0.087	0.149	0.338	0.431	0.082
25	0.182	0.370	0.358	0.090	0.166	0.262	0.351	0.221
26	0.338	0.304	0.274	0.084	0.218	0.221	0.367	0.194
27	0.183	0.319	0.407	0.091	0.253	0.230	0.197	0.321
28	0.317	0.229	0.339	0.115	0.262	0.219	0.315	0.204
29	0.255	0.306	0.345	0.095	0.225	0.233	0.307	0.235
30	0.255	0.306	0.345	0.095	0.225	0.233	0.307	0.235
31	0.255	0.306	0.345	0.095	0.225	0.233	0.307	0.235
32	0.255	0.306	0.345	0.095	0.225	0.233	0.307	0.235
33	0.255	0.306	0.345	0.095	0.225	0.233	0.307	0.235
34	0.255	0.306	0.345	0.095	0.225	0.233	0.307	0.235
35	0.255	0.306	0.345	0.095	0.225	0.233	0.307	0.235
36	0.255	0.306	0.345	0.095	0.225	0.233	0.307	0.235
37	0.255	0.306	0.345	0.095	0.225	0.233	0.307	0.235
38	0.255	0.306	0.345	0.095	0.225	0.233	0.307	0.235
39	0.000	0.000	1.000	0.000	0.000	0.000	1.000	0.000

Table E.1 (continued)

d. From College Year 4

	From College Year 4				
Age	Stay in C4	Advance to Grad 1	Exit to Some Col	Exit to AD	Exit to BD
12	0.275	0.075	0.046	0.209	0.395
13	0.275	0.075	0.046	0.209	0.395
14	0.275	0.075	0.046	0.209	0.395
15	0.275	0.075	0.046	0.209	0.395
16	0.275	0.075	0.046	0.209	0.395
17	0.275	0.075	0.046	0.209	0.395
18	0.275	0.075	0.046	0.209	0.395
19	0.275	0.075	0.046	0.209	0.395
20	0.275	0.075	0.046	0.209	0.395
21	0.200	0.084	0.258	0.028	0.430
22	0.172	0.057	0.209	0.040	0.523
23	0.203	0.060	0.157	0.092	0.488
24	0.192	0.058	0.195	0.023	0.533
25	0.268	0.000	0.000	0.307	0.425
26	0.212	0.074	0.252	0.049	0.412
27	0.224	0.000	0.000	0.373	0.403
28	0.359	0.000	0.000	0.320	0.322
29	0.265	0.022	0.000	0.322	0.391
30	0.265	0.022	0.000	0.322	0.391
31	0.265	0.022	0.000	0.322	0.391
32	0.265	0.022	0.000	0.322	0.391
33	0.265	0.022	0.000	0.322	0.391
34	0.265	0.022	0.000	0.322	0.391
35	0.265	0.022	0.000	0.322	0.391
36	0.265	0.022	0.000	0.322	0.391
37	0.265	0.022	0.000	0.322	0.391
38	0.265	0.022	0.000	0.322	0.391
39	0.000	0.000	1.000	0.000	0.000

Table E.1 (continued)

e. From Grad School Year 1, Grad School Year 2+

	From Grad School Year 1				From Grad School Year 2+		
Age	Stay in Grad 1	Advance to Grad 2+	Exit to BD	Exit to GD	Stay in Grad 2+	Exit to BD	Exit to GD
12	0.169	0.320	0.455	0.056	0.831	0.000	0.169
13	0.169	0.320	0.455	0.056	0.831	0.000	0.169
14	0.169	0.320	0.455	0.056	0.831	0.000	0.169
15	0.169	0.320	0.455	0.056	0.831	0.000	0.169
16	0.169	0.320	0.455	0.056	0.831	0.000	0.169
17	0.169	0.320	0.455	0.056	0.831	0.000	0.169
18	0.169	0.320	0.455	0.056	0.831	0.000	0.169
19	0.169	0.320	0.455	0.056	0.831	0.000	0.169
20	0.169	0.320	0.455	0.056	0.831	0.000	0.169
21	0.169	0.320	0.455	0.056	0.831	0.000	0.169
22	0.151	0.395	0.410	0.045	0.849	0.000	0.151
23	0.212	0.334	0.406	0.048	0.788	0.000	0.212
24	0.207	0.365	0.389	0.039	0.793	0.000	0.207
25	0.173	0.426	0.353	0.048	0.827	0.000	0.173
26	0.266	0.339	0.334	0.061	0.734	0.000	0.266
27	0.239	0.344	0.364	0.052	0.761	0.000	0.239
28	0.185	0.355	0.349	0.111	0.815	0.000	0.185
29	0.216	0.366	0.350	0.068	0.784	0.000	0.216
30	0.216	0.366	0.350	0.068	0.784	0.000	0.216
31	0.216	0.366	0.350	0.068	0.784	0.000	0.216
32	0.216	0.366	0.350	0.068	0.784	0.000	0.216
33	0.216	0.366	0.350	0.068	0.784	0.000	0.216
34	0.216	0.366	0.350	0.068	0.784	0.000	0.216
35	0.216	0.366	0.350	0.068	0.784	0.000	0.216
36	0.216	0.366	0.350	0.068	0.784	0.000	0.216
37	0.216	0.366	0.350	0.068	0.784	0.000	0.216
38	0.216	0.366	0.350	0.068	0.784	0.000	0.216
39	0.000	0.000	1.000	0.000	0.000	1.000	0.000

Table E.2

Annual Flow Rates Within and Out of Schools for Native-Born Non-Hispanic White Males in California, by Age and Grade

a. From 9th, 10th, and 11th Grade

	From 9th Grade			From 10th Grade			From 11th Grade		
Age	Stay in 9th	Advance to 10th	Exit to Some HS	Stay in 10th	Advance to 11th	Exit to Some HS	Stay in 11th	Advance to 12th	Exit to Some HS
12	0.000	1.000	0.000	0.043	0.957	0.000	0.034	0.966	0.000
13	0.000	1.000	0.000	0.043	0.957	0.000	0.034	0.966	0.000
14	0.016	0.984	0.000	0.043	0.957	0.000	0.034	0.966	0.000
15	0.041	0.959	0.000	0.017	0.983	0.000	0.034	0.966	0.000
16	0.055	0.945	0.000	0.024	0.976	0.000	0.008	0.992	0.000
17	0.080	0.920	0.000	0.037	0.963	0.000	0.017	0.983	0.000
18	0.080	0.920	0.000	0.037	0.963	0.000	0.029	0.971	0.000
19	0.080	0.920	0.000	0.037	0.963	0.000	0.053	0.947	0.000
20	0.080	0.920	0.000	0.037	0.963	0.000	0.053	0.947	0.000
21	0.080	0.920	0.000	0.037	0.963	0.000	0.053	0.947	0.000
22	0.080	0.920	0.000	0.037	0.963	0.000	0.053	0.947	0.000
23	0.080	0.920	0.000	0.037	0.963	0.000	0.053	0.947	0.000
24	0.080	0.920	0.000	0.037	0.963	0.000	0.053	0.947	0.000
25	0.080	0.920	0.000	0.037	0.963	0.000	0.053	0.947	0.000
26	0.080	0.920	0.000	0.037	0.963	0.000	0.053	0.947	0.000
27	0.080	0.920	0.000	0.037	0.963	0.000	0.053	0.947	0.000
28	0.080	0.920	0.000	0.037	0.963	0.000	0.053	0.947	0.000
29	0.080	0.920	0.000	0.037	0.963	0.000	0.053	0.947	0.000
30	0.080	0.920	0.000	0.037	0.963	0.000	0.053	0.947	0.000
31	0.080	0.920	0.000	0.037	0.963	0.000	0.053	0.947	0.000
32	0.080	0.920	0.000	0.037	0.963	0.000	0.053	0.947	0.000
33	0.080	0.920	0.000	0.037	0.963	0.000	0.053	0.947	0.000
34	0.080	0.920	0.000	0.037	0.963	0.000	0.053	0.947	0.000
35	0.080	0.920	0.000	0.037	0.963	0.000	0.053	0.947	0.000
36	0.080	0.920	0.000	0.037	0.963	0.000	0.053	0.947	0.000
37	0.080	0.920	0.000	0.037	0.963	0.000	0.053	0.947	0.000
38	0.080	0.920	0.000	0.037	0.963	0.000	0.053	0.947	0.000
39	0.000	0.000	1.000	0.000	0.000	1.000	0.000	0.000	1.000

Table E.2 (continued)

b. From 12th Grade, College Year 1

Age	From 12th Grade					From College Year 1		
	Stay in 12th	Advance to College	Exit to Some HS	Exit to 12th ND	Exit to HSD	Stay in C1	Advance to C2	Exit to Some Col
12	0.057	0.776	0.011	0.004	0.152	0.122	0.556	0.322
13	0.057	0.776	0.011	0.004	0.152	0.122	0.556	0.322
14	0.057	0.776	0.011	0.004	0.152	0.122	0.556	0.322
15	0.057	0.776	0.011	0.004	0.152	0.122	0.556	0.322
16	0.057	0.776	0.011	0.004	0.152	0.122	0.556	0.322
17	0.021	0.740	0.005	0.011	0.224	0.122	0.556	0.322
18	0.043	0.538	0.016	0.015	0.388	0.077	0.606	0.318
19	0.081	0.411	0.064	0.034	0.410	0.093	0.528	0.379
20	0.054	0.245	0.084	0.046	0.571	0.134	0.455	0.411
21	0.054	0.245	0.084	0.046	0.571	0.121	0.450	0.429
22	0.054	0.245	0.084	0.046	0.571	0.165	0.429	0.406
23	0.054	0.245	0.084	0.046	0.571	0.135	0.429	0.436
24	0.054	0.245	0.084	0.046	0.571	0.165	0.386	0.449
25	0.054	0.245	0.084	0.046	0.571	0.194	0.298	0.508
26	0.054	0.245	0.084	0.046	0.571	0.193	0.271	0.536
27	0.054	0.245	0.084	0.046	0.571	0.156	0.338	0.506
28	0.054	0.245	0.084	0.046	0.571	0.178	0.375	0.447
29	0.054	0.245	0.084	0.046	0.571	0.180	0.320	0.499
30	0.054	0.245	0.084	0.046	0.571	0.180	0.320	0.499
31	0.054	0.245	0.084	0.046	0.571	0.180	0.320	0.499
32	0.054	0.245	0.084	0.046	0.571	0.180	0.320	0.499
33	0.054	0.245	0.084	0.046	0.571	0.180	0.320	0.499
34	0.054	0.245	0.084	0.046	0.571	0.180	0.320	0.499
35	0.054	0.245	0.084	0.046	0.571	0.180	0.320	0.499
36	0.054	0.245	0.084	0.046	0.571	0.180	0.320	0.499
37	0.054	0.245	0.084	0.046	0.571	0.180	0.320	0.499
38	0.054	0.245	0.084	0.046	0.571	0.180	0.320	0.499
39	0.000	0.000	1.000	0.000	0.000	0.000	0.000	1.000

Table E.2 (continued)

c. From College Year 2, College Year 3

	From College Year 2				From College Year 3			
Age	Stay in C2	Advance to C3	Exit to Some Col	Exit to AD	Stay in C3	Advance to C4	Exit to Some Col	Exit to AD
12	0.131	0.579	0.260	0.031	0.145	0.592	0.221	0.042
13	0.131	0.579	0.260	0.031	0.145	0.592	0.221	0.042
14	0.131	0.579	0.260	0.031	0.145	0.592	0.221	0.042
15	0.131	0.579	0.260	0.031	0.145	0.592	0.221	0.042
16	0.131	0.579	0.260	0.031	0.145	0.592	0.221	0.042
17	0.131	0.579	0.260	0.031	0.145	0.592	0.221	0.042
18	0.131	0.579	0.260	0.031	0.145	0.592	0.221	0.042
19	0.091	0.598	0.282	0.029	0.145	0.592	0.221	0.042
20	0.094	0.553	0.289	0.064	0.050	0.690	0.246	0.014
21	0.107	0.509	0.329	0.055	0.071	0.606	0.301	0.021
22	0.132	0.416	0.374	0.078	0.100	0.564	0.304	0.031
23	0.146	0.421	0.324	0.110	0.103	0.527	0.316	0.054
24	0.127	0.420	0.327	0.126	0.128	0.565	0.264	0.043
25	0.142	0.360	0.367	0.131	0.143	0.438	0.303	0.117
26	0.264	0.296	0.317	0.123	0.187	0.370	0.341	0.102
27	0.143	0.310	0.415	0.132	0.217	0.384	0.229	0.170
28	0.248	0.223	0.362	0.167	0.225	0.367	0.300	0.108
29	0.199	0.297	0.365	0.138	0.193	0.390	0.293	0.124
30	0.199	0.297	0.365	0.138	0.193	0.390	0.293	0.124
31	0.199	0.297	0.365	0.138	0.193	0.390	0.293	0.124
32	0.199	0.297	0.365	0.138	0.193	0.390	0.293	0.124
33	0.199	0.297	0.365	0.138	0.193	0.390	0.293	0.124
34	0.199	0.297	0.365	0.138	0.193	0.390	0.293	0.124
35	0.199	0.297	0.365	0.138	0.193	0.390	0.293	0.124
36	0.199	0.297	0.365	0.138	0.193	0.390	0.293	0.124
37	0.199	0.297	0.365	0.138	0.193	0.390	0.293	0.124
38	0.199	0.297	0.365	0.138	0.193	0.390	0.293	0.124
39	0.000	0.000	1.000	0.000	0.000	0.000	1.000	0.000

Table E.2 (continued)

d. From College Year 4

	From College Year 4				
Age	Stay in C4	Advance to Grad 1	Exit to Some Col	Exit to AD	Exit to BD
12	0.204	0.290	0.010	0.038	0.459
13	0.204	0.290	0.010	0.038	0.459
14	0.204	0.290	0.010	0.038	0.459
15	0.204	0.290	0.010	0.038	0.459
16	0.204	0.290	0.010	0.038	0.459
17	0.204	0.290	0.010	0.038	0.459
18	0.204	0.290	0.010	0.038	0.459
19	0.204	0.290	0.010	0.038	0.459
20	0.204	0.290	0.010	0.038	0.459
21	0.148	0.323	0.024	0.005	0.499
22	0.127	0.217	0.041	0.007	0.607
23	0.150	0.230	0.036	0.017	0.566
24	0.142	0.222	0.013	0.004	0.619
25	0.198	0.121	0.115	0.072	0.494
26	0.157	0.285	0.071	0.009	0.478
27	0.166	0.171	0.111	0.083	0.468
28	0.265	0.140	0.153	0.068	0.374
29	0.197	0.179	0.113	0.058	0.454
30	0.197	0.179	0.113	0.058	0.454
31	0.197	0.179	0.113	0.058	0.454
32	0.197	0.179	0.113	0.058	0.454
33	0.197	0.179	0.113	0.058	0.454
34	0.197	0.179	0.113	0.058	0.454
35	0.197	0.179	0.113	0.058	0.454
36	0.197	0.179	0.113	0.058	0.454
37	0.197	0.179	0.113	0.058	0.454
38	0.197	0.179	0.113	0.058	0.454
39	0.000	0.000	1.000	0.000	0.000

Table E.2 (continued)

e. From Grad School Year 1, Grad School Year 2+

| Age | From Grad School Year 1 | | | | From Grad School Year 2+ | | |
	Stay in Grad 1	Advance to Grad 2+	Exit to BD	Exit to GD	Stay in Grad 2+	Exit to BD	Exit to GD
12	0.217	0.423	0.291	0.069	0.564	0.095	0.345
13	0.217	0.423	0.291	0.069	0.564	0.095	0.345
14	0.217	0.423	0.291	0.069	0.564	0.095	0.345
15	0.217	0.423	0.291	0.069	0.564	0.095	0.345
16	0.217	0.423	0.291	0.069	0.564	0.095	0.345
17	0.217	0.423	0.291	0.069	0.564	0.095	0.345
18	0.217	0.423	0.291	0.069	0.564	0.095	0.345
19	0.217	0.423	0.291	0.069	0.564	0.095	0.345
20	0.217	0.423	0.291	0.069	0.564	0.095	0.345
21	0.217	0.423	0.291	0.069	0.564	0.095	0.345
22	0.193	0.522	0.230	0.055	0.564	0.095	0.345
23	0.271	0.442	0.228	0.058	0.662	0.045	0.296
24	0.264	0.483	0.205	0.048	0.656	0.024	0.324
25	0.222	0.563	0.156	0.059	0.530	0.045	0.431
26	0.340	0.448	0.137	0.075	0.517	0.000	0.490
27	0.306	0.456	0.174	0.064	0.539	0.121	0.344
28	0.236	0.470	0.157	0.136	0.476	0.115	0.415
29	0.276	0.484	0.156	0.083	0.515	0.070	0.420
30	0.276	0.484	0.156	0.083	0.515	0.070	0.420
31	0.276	0.484	0.156	0.083	0.515	0.070	0.420
32	0.276	0.484	0.156	0.083	0.515	0.070	0.420
33	0.276	0.484	0.156	0.083	0.515	0.070	0.420
34	0.276	0.484	0.156	0.083	0.515	0.070	0.420
35	0.276	0.484	0.156	0.083	0.515	0.070	0.420
36	0.276	0.484	0.156	0.083	0.515	0.070	0.420
37	0.276	0.484	0.156	0.083	0.515	0.070	0.420
38	0.276	0.484	0.156	0.083	0.515	0.070	0.420
39	0.000	0.000	1.000	0.000	0.000	1.000	0.000

Table E.3

Annual Flow Rates from Not in School to School for Native-Born Mexican Males in California, by Age and Level of Education

a. From 8th Grade or Less, Some High School, 12th Grade ND, High School Degree

Age	From 8th Grade or Less		From Some High School				From 12th Grade No Degree		From High School Degree	
	Stay Out of School	to 9th	Stay Out of School	to 10th	to 11th	to 12th	Stay Out of School	to 12th	Stay Out of School	to C1
12	0.961	0.039	1.000	0.000	0.000	0.000	1.000	0.000	1.000	0.000
13	0.502	0.498	1.000	0.000	0.000	0.000	1.000	0.000	1.000	0.000
14	0.381	0.619	0.536	0.348	0.103	0.013	1.000	0.000	1.000	0.000
15	0.478	0.522	0.487	0.113	0.304	0.096	1.000	0.000	1.000	0.000
16	0.757	0.243	0.568	0.047	0.107	0.278	0.290	0.710	0.794	0.206
17	0.942	0.058	0.857	0.012	0.032	0.100	0.693	0.307	0.774	0.226
18	0.980	0.020	0.944	0.005	0.013	0.037	0.829	0.171	0.890	0.110
19	0.976	0.024	0.975	0.001	0.004	0.020	0.923	0.077	0.930	0.070
20	0.973	0.027	0.980	0.001	0.002	0.017	0.943	0.057	0.943	0.057
21	1.000	0.000	0.986	0.002	0.004	0.007	0.985	0.015	0.951	0.049
22	0.988	0.012	0.978	0.002	0.006	0.013	0.977	0.023	0.963	0.037
23	0.991	0.009	0.977	0.002	0.008	0.013	0.966	0.034	0.967	0.033
24	0.994	0.006	0.988	0.002	0.003	0.006	0.997	0.003	0.975	0.025
25	0.997	0.003	0.992	0.002	0.001	0.005	0.982	0.018	0.977	0.023
26	0.997	0.003	0.992	0.002	0.001	0.005	0.982	0.018	0.983	0.017
27	0.997	0.003	0.986	0.002	0.004	0.008	0.982	0.018	0.983	0.017
28	0.997	0.003	0.988	0.002	0.001	0.009	0.982	0.018	0.984	0.016
29	0.997	0.003	0.989	0.002	0.002	0.007	0.982	0.018	1.000	0.000
30	0.997	0.003	0.989	0.002	0.002	0.007	0.982	0.018	1.000	0.000
31	0.997	0.003	0.989	0.002	0.002	0.007	0.982	0.018	1.000	0.000
32	0.997	0.003	0.989	0.002	0.002	0.007	0.982	0.018	1.000	0.000
33	0.997	0.003	0.989	0.002	0.002	0.007	0.982	0.018	1.000	0.000
34	0.997	0.003	0.989	0.002	0.002	0.007	0.982	0.018	1.000	0.000
35	0.997	0.003	0.989	0.002	0.002	0.007	0.982	0.018	1.000	0.000
36	0.997	0.003	0.989	0.002	0.002	0.007	0.982	0.018	1.000	0.000
37	0.997	0.003	0.989	0.002	0.002	0.007	0.982	0.018	1.000	0.000
38	0.997	0.003	0.989	0.002	0.002	0.007	0.982	0.018	1.000	0.000
39	1.000	0.000	1.000	0.000	0.000	0.000	1.000	0.000	1.000	0.000

Table E.3 (continued)

b. From Some College, Associate Degree

Age	From Some College				From AD		
	Stay Out of School	to C2	to C3	to C4	Stay Out of School	to C2	to C3
12	1.000	0.000	0.000	0.000	1.000	0.000	0.000
13	1.000	0.000	0.000	0.000	1.000	0.000	0.000
14	1.000	0.000	0.000	0.000	1.000	0.000	0.000
15	1.000	0.000	0.000	0.000	1.000	0.000	0.000
16	1.000	0.000	0.000	0.000	1.000	0.000	0.000
17	0.910	0.090	0.000	0.000	1.000	0.000	0.000
18	0.661	0.291	0.042	0.005	0.946	0.000	0.054
19	0.767	0.166	0.061	0.006	0.861	0.000	0.139
20	0.832	0.070	0.080	0.018	0.922	0.000	0.078
21	0.896	0.034	0.050	0.020	0.947	0.000	0.053
22	0.920	0.045	0.026	0.009	0.954	0.000	0.046
23	0.940	0.025	0.029	0.006	0.947	0.000	0.053
24	0.948	0.027	0.019	0.006	0.984	0.000	0.016
25	0.967	0.023	0.006	0.004	0.976	0.000	0.024
26	0.969	0.020	0.010	0.001	0.974	0.000	0.026
27	0.978	0.013	0.006	0.003	0.987	0.000	0.013
28	0.975	0.013	0.011	0.001	0.976	0.000	0.024
29	0.972	0.017	0.008	0.002	0.978	0.000	0.022
30	0.972	0.017	0.008	0.002	0.978	0.000	0.022
31	0.972	0.017	0.008	0.002	0.978	0.000	0.022
32	0.972	0.017	0.008	0.002	0.978	0.000	0.022
33	0.972	0.017	0.008	0.002	0.978	0.000	0.022
34	0.972	0.017	0.008	0.002	0.978	0.000	0.022
35	0.972	0.017	0.008	0.002	0.978	0.000	0.022
36	0.972	0.017	0.008	0.002	0.978	0.000	0.022
37	0.972	0.017	0.008	0.002	0.978	0.000	0.022
38	0.972	0.017	0.008	0.002	0.978	0.000	0.022
39	1.000	0.000	0.000	0.000	1.000	0.000	0.000

Table E.3 (continued)

c. From Bachelor's Degree, Graduate Degree

Age	From BD		From GD	
	Stay Out of School	to G1	Stay Out of School	to G2+
12	1.000	0.000	1.000	0.000
13	1.000	0.000	1.000	0.000
14	1.000	0.000	1.000	0.000
15	1.000	0.000	1.000	0.000
16	1.000	0.000	1.000	0.000
17	1.000	0.000	1.000	0.000
18	1.000	0.000	1.000	0.000
19	1.000	0.000	1.000	0.000
20	0.717	0.283	1.000	0.000
21	0.922	0.078	1.000	0.000
22	0.875	0.125	0.746	0.254
23	0.902	0.098	0.717	0.283
24	0.920	0.080	0.360	0.640
25	0.945	0.055	0.653	0.347
26	0.945	0.055	0.807	0.193
27	0.947	0.053	0.710	0.290
28	0.967	0.033	0.788	0.212
29	0.951	0.049	0.739	0.261
30	0.951	0.049	0.739	0.261
31	0.951	0.049	0.739	0.261
32	0.951	0.049	0.739	0.261
33	0.951	0.049	0.739	0.261
34	0.951	0.049	0.739	0.261
35	0.951	0.049	0.739	0.261
36	0.951	0.049	0.739	0.261
37	0.951	0.049	0.739	0.261
38	0.951	0.049	0.739	0.261
39	1.000	0.000	1.000	0.000

Table E.4

Annual Flow Rates from Not in School to School for Native-Born Non-Hispanic White Males in California, by Age and Level of Education

a. From 8th Grade or Less, Some High School, 12th Grade ND, High School Degree

Age	From 8th Grade or Less		From Some High School				From 12th Grade No Degree		From High School Degree	
	Stay Out of School	to 9th	Stay Out of School	to 10th	to 11th	to 12th	Stay Out of School	to 12th	Stay Out of School	to C1
12	0.687	0.313	1.000	0.000	0.000	0.000	1.000	0.000	1.000	0.000
13	0.000	1.000	1.000	0.000	0.000	0.000	1.000	0.000	1.000	0.000
14	0.000	1.000	0.022	0.787	0.172	0.018	1.000	0.000	1.000	0.000
15	0.000	1.000	0.101	0.256	0.508	0.135	1.000	0.000	1.000	0.000
16	0.000	1.000	0.323	0.105	0.179	0.393	0.212	0.788	0.697	0.303
17	0.525	0.475	0.779	0.027	0.053	0.141	0.659	0.341	0.668	0.332
18	0.835	0.165	0.913	0.012	0.022	0.053	0.810	0.190	0.838	0.162
19	0.807	0.193	0.963	0.002	0.007	0.028	0.915	0.085	0.897	0.103
20	0.778	0.222	0.970	0.003	0.003	0.024	0.937	0.063	0.917	0.083
21	1.000	0.000	0.978	0.005	0.007	0.010	0.983	0.017	0.928	0.072
22	0.902	0.098	0.966	0.005	0.011	0.019	0.974	0.026	0.945	0.055
23	0.930	0.070	0.963	0.005	0.014	0.018	0.962	0.038	0.951	0.049
24	0.950	0.050	0.981	0.005	0.005	0.009	0.997	0.003	0.964	0.036
25	0.976	0.024	0.987	0.005	0.001	0.007	0.980	0.020	0.966	0.034
26	0.976	0.024	0.986	0.005	0.002	0.007	0.980	0.020	0.975	0.025
27	0.976	0.024	0.977	0.005	0.007	0.012	0.980	0.020	0.975	0.025
28	0.976	0.024	0.981	0.005	0.002	0.012	0.980	0.020	0.977	0.023
29	0.976	0.024	0.983	0.005	0.003	0.009	0.980	0.020	1.000	0.000
30	0.976	0.024	0.983	0.005	0.003	0.009	0.980	0.020	1.000	0.000
31	0.976	0.024	0.983	0.005	0.003	0.009	0.980	0.020	1.000	0.000
32	0.976	0.024	0.983	0.005	0.003	0.009	0.980	0.020	1.000	0.000
33	0.976	0.024	0.983	0.005	0.003	0.009	0.980	0.020	1.000	0.000
34	0.976	0.024	0.983	0.005	0.003	0.009	0.980	0.020	1.000	0.000
35	0.976	0.024	0.983	0.005	0.003	0.009	0.980	0.020	1.000	0.000
36	0.976	0.024	0.983	0.005	0.003	0.009	0.980	0.020	1.000	0.000
37	0.976	0.024	0.983	0.005	0.003	0.009	0.980	0.020	1.000	0.000
38	0.976	0.024	0.983	0.005	0.003	0.009	0.980	0.020	1.000	0.000
39	1.000	0.000	1.000	0.000	0.000	0.000	1.000	0.000	1.000	0.000

Table E.4 (continued)

b. From Some College, Associate Degree

Age	From Some College				From AD		
	Stay Out of School	to C2	to C3	to C4	Stay Out of School	to C2	to C3
12	1.000	0.000	0.000	0.000	1.000	0.000	0.000
13	1.000	0.000	0.000	0.000	1.000	0.000	0.000
14	1.000	0.000	0.000	0.000	1.000	0.000	0.000
15	1.000	0.000	0.000	0.000	1.000	0.000	0.000
16	1.000	0.000	0.000	0.000	1.000	0.000	0.000
17	0.913	0.087	0.000	0.000	1.000	0.000	0.000
18	0.663	0.283	0.045	0.009	0.931	0.031	0.038
19	0.764	0.161	0.065	0.010	0.878	0.024	0.098
20	0.818	0.068	0.084	0.029	0.945	0.000	0.055
21	0.882	0.033	0.053	0.032	0.944	0.019	0.038
22	0.914	0.044	0.028	0.014	0.957	0.011	0.032
23	0.935	0.024	0.031	0.010	0.957	0.006	0.037
24	0.944	0.026	0.020	0.009	0.983	0.006	0.012
25	0.965	0.023	0.006	0.006	0.975	0.009	0.017
26	0.968	0.019	0.011	0.002	0.977	0.005	0.018
27	0.976	0.012	0.007	0.005	0.982	0.008	0.009
28	0.974	0.013	0.011	0.002	0.977	0.006	0.017
29	0.971	0.017	0.009	0.004	0.978	0.007	0.015
30	0.971	0.017	0.009	0.004	0.978	0.007	0.015
31	0.971	0.017	0.009	0.004	0.978	0.007	0.015
32	0.971	0.017	0.009	0.004	0.978	0.007	0.015
33	0.971	0.017	0.009	0.004	0.978	0.007	0.015
34	0.971	0.017	0.009	0.004	0.978	0.007	0.015
35	0.971	0.017	0.009	0.004	0.978	0.007	0.015
36	0.971	0.017	0.009	0.004	0.978	0.007	0.015
37	0.971	0.017	0.009	0.004	0.978	0.007	0.015
38	0.971	0.017	0.009	0.004	0.978	0.007	0.015
39	1.000	0.000	0.000	0.000	1.000	0.000	0.000

Table E.4 (continued)

c. From Bachelor's Degree, Graduate Degree

	From BD		From GD	
Age	Stay Out of School	to G1	Stay Out of School	to G2+
12	1.000	0.000	1.000	0.000
13	1.000	0.000	1.000	0.000
14	1.000	0.000	1.000	0.000
15	1.000	0.000	1.000	0.000
16	1.000	0.000	1.000	0.000
17	1.000	0.000	1.000	0.000
18	1.000	0.000	1.000	0.000
19	1.000	0.000	1.000	0.000
20	0.777	0.223	1.000	0.000
21	0.939	0.061	1.000	0.000
22	0.901	0.099	0.956	0.044
23	0.923	0.077	0.951	0.049
24	0.937	0.063	0.889	0.111
25	0.957	0.043	0.940	0.060
26	0.956	0.044	0.967	0.033
27	0.958	0.042	0.950	0.050
28	0.974	0.026	0.963	0.037
29	0.961	0.039	0.955	0.045
30	0.961	0.039	0.955	0.045
31	0.961	0.039	0.955	0.045
32	0.961	0.039	0.955	0.045
33	0.961	0.039	0.955	0.045
34	0.961	0.039	0.955	0.045
35	0.961	0.039	0.955	0.045
36	0.961	0.039	0.955	0.045
37	0.961	0.039	0.955	0.045
38	0.961	0.039	0.955	0.045
39	1.000	0.000	1.000	0.000

ANNUAL FLOWS FOR BIRTHS, DEATHS, AND IMMIGRATION

The four tables in this appendix contain the demographic in- and outflows programmed in the RAND Education Simulation Model. Table F.1 shows the number of births per year (from 1990 to 2015) by ethnicity and gender; Table F.2 displays the number of deaths per year by age, ethnicity, and gender. Table F.3 shows the annual number of immigrants by age, ethnicity, and gender; Table F.4 displays the annual number of immigrants by age, gender, and education at time of arrival in the United States.

Table F.1

Births by Year, Ethnicity, and Gender

a. White Non-Hispanics, Black Non-Hispanics, and Asian/Pacific Islanders

Year	White Non-Hispanics			Black Non-Hispanics			Asian/Pacific Islanders		
	Men	Women	Total	Men	Women	Total	Men	Women	Total
1990	1,267,777	1,203,941	2,471,718	297,198	290,034	587,232	81,030	77,888	158,918
1991	1,267,777	1,203,941	2,471,718	297,198	290,034	587,232	81,030	77,888	158,918
1992	1,267,777	1,203,941	2,471,718	297,198	290,034	587,232	81,030	77,888	158,918
1993	1,267,777	1,203,941	2,471,718	297,198	290,034	587,232	81,030	77,888	158,918
1994	1,267,777	1,203,941	2,471,718	297,198	290,034	587,232	81,030	77,888	158,918
1995	1,267,777	1,203,941	2,471,718	297,198	290,034	587,232	81,030	77,888	158,918
1996	1,247,569	1,184,774	2,432,343	297,426	290,059	587,485	83,138	79,961	163,099
1997	1,229,617	1,167,689	2,397,306	298,172	290,587	588,759	85,239	82,030	167,269
1998	1,214,090	1,152,894	2,366,984	299,368	291,555	590,923	87,339	84,104	171,443
1999	1,200,470	1,139,968	2,340,438	300,752	292,725	593,477	89,441	86,183	175,624
2000	1,189,134	1,129,138	2,318,272	302,374	294,086	596,460	91,501	88,234	179,735
2001	1,179,782	1,120,236	2,300,018	304,131	295,599	599,730	93,594	90,312	183,906
2002	1,172,743	1,113,472	2,286,215	306,110	297,332	603,442	95,678	92,382	188,060
2003	1,167,954	1,108,806	2,276,760	308,481	299,409	607,890	97,816	94,509	192,325
2004	1,165,382	1,106,313	2,271,695	311,229	301,884	613,113	100,015	96,697	196,712
2005	1,165,793	1,106,579	2,272,372	314,674	305,011	619,685	102,307	98,980	201,287
2006	1,167,837	1,108,488	2,276,325	318,517	308,536	627,053	104,722	101,375	206,097
2007	1,172,183	1,112,375	2,284,558	322,746	312,410	635,156	107,245	103,874	211,119
2008	1,178,021	1,117,776	2,295,797	327,126	316,411	643,537	109,879	106,481	216,360
2009	1,184,415	1,123,697	2,308,112	331,242	320,161	651,403	112,612	109,181	221,793
2010	1,190,821	1,129,656	2,320,477	335,203	323,727	658,930	115,399	111,934	227,333
2011	1,196,607	1,134,963	2,331,570	338,763	326,910	665,673	118,266	114,763	233,029
2012	1,201,739	1,139,610	2,341,349	341,971	329,743	671,714	121,146	117,602	238,748
2013	1,205,940	1,143,428	2,349,368	344,917	332,351	677,268	124,078	120,495	244,573
2014	1,208,869	1,146,124	2,354,993	347,528	334,633	682,161	127,042	123,416	250,458
2015	1,211,076	1,148,056	2,359,132	350,078	336,872	686,950	130,020	126,359	256,379

Table F.1 (continued)

b. Mexicans, Other Hispanics, and All Groups

Year	Mexicans			Other Hispanics			All Groups		
	Men	Women	Total	Men	Women	Total	Men	Women	Total
1990	152,699	146,570	299,270	151,864	145,768	297,631	1,950,568	1,864,201	3,814,769
1991	152,699	146,570	299,270	151,864	145,768	297,631	1,950,568	1,864,201	3,814,769
1992	152,699	146,570	299,270	151,864	145,768	297,631	1,950,568	1,864,201	3,814,769
1993	152,699	146,570	299,270	151,864	145,768	297,631	1,950,568	1,864,201	3,814,769
1994	152,699	146,570	299,270	151,864	145,768	297,631	1,950,568	1,864,201	3,814,769
1995	152,699	146,570	299,270	151,864	145,768	297,631	1,950,568	1,864,201	3,814,769
1996	155,812	149,495	305,307	154,959	148,677	303,636	1,938,904	1,852,966	3,791,870
1997	159,065	152,567	311,632	158,194	151,732	309,926	1,930,287	1,844,605	3,774,892
1998	162,511	155,830	318,341	161,622	154,977	316,599	1,924,930	1,839,360	3,764,290
1999	166,110	159,240	325,350	165,200	158,368	323,568	1,921,973	1,836,484	3,758,457
2000	169,823	162,769	332,592	168,894	161,878	330,772	1,921,726	1,836,105	3,757,831
2001	173,713	166,458	340,171	172,763	165,546	338,309	1,923,983	1,838,151	3,762,134
2002	177,720	170,263	347,983	176,748	169,331	346,079	1,928,999	1,842,780	3,771,779
2003	181,916	174,240	356,156	180,920	173,287	354,207	1,937,087	1,850,251	3,787,338
2004	186,338	178,434	364,772	185,317	177,458	362,775	1,948,281	1,860,786	3,809,067
2005	191,062	182,923	373,985	190,016	181,922	371,938	1,963,852	1,875,415	3,839,267
2006	196,188	187,784	383,972	195,114	186,757	381,871	1,982,378	1,892,940	3,875,318
2007	201,745	193,057	394,802	200,641	192,000	392,641	2,004,560	1,913,716	3,918,276
2008	207,760	198,765	406,524	206,622	197,676	404,299	2,029,408	1,937,109	3,966,517
2009	214,087	204,763	418,850	212,916	203,642	416,558	2,055,272	1,961,444	4,016,716
2010	220,532	210,877	431,409	219,325	209,723	429,048	2,081,280	1,985,917	4,067,197
2011	226,965	216,964	443,929	225,722	215,776	441,498	2,106,323	2,009,376	4,115,699
2012	233,160	222,823	455,984	231,884	221,604	453,487	2,129,900	2,031,382	4,161,282
2013	239,087	228,424	467,511	237,779	227,173	464,952	2,151,801	2,051,871	4,203,672
2014	244,718	233,738	478,456	243,378	232,458	475,836	2,171,535	2,070,369	4,241,904
2015	250,106	238,818	488,924	248,737	237,511	486,248	2,190,017	2,087,616	4,277,633

Table F.2

Annual Death Rates by Age, Ethnicity, and Gender (percent)

Age	White Non-Hispanics		Black Non-Hispanics		Asian/Pacific Islanders		Mexicans		Other Hispanics	
	Men	Women	Men	Women	Men	Women	Men	Women	Men	Women
1	0.60	0.44	1.69	1.14	0.37	0.33	0.79	0.70	0.79	0.70
2	0.09	0.07	0.19	0.16	0.07	0.07	0.12	0.10	0.12	0.10
3	0.06	0.05	0.14	0.11	0.05	0.05	0.08	0.07	0.08	0.07
4	0.05	0.04	0.10	0.09	0.04	0.03	0.06	0.05	0.06	0.05
5	0.04	0.03	0.09	0.07	0.03	0.03	0.05	0.04	0.05	0.04
6	0.03	0.02	0.07	0.05	0.03	0.02	0.04	0.03	0.04	0.03
7	0.03	0.02	0.05	0.04	0.02	0.02	0.03	0.02	0.03	0.02
8	0.02	0.02	0.04	0.03	0.02	0.01	0.03	0.02	0.03	0.02
9	0.02	0.01	0.03	0.02	0.02	0.01	0.02	0.01	0.02	0.01
10	0.01	0.01	0.02	0.02	0.02	0.01	0.01	0.01	0.01	0.01
11	0.01	0.01	0.01	0.02	0.02	0.01	0.01	0.01	0.01	0.01
12	0.01	0.01	0.01	0.02	0.02	0.01	0.01	0.01	0.00	0.01
13	0.02	0.01	0.02	0.03	0.02	0.01	0.01	0.02	0.01	0.02
14	0.03	0.02	0.05	0.03	0.02	0.01	0.03	0.02	0.03	0.02
15	0.05	0.02	0.09	0.03	0.03	0.01	0.06	0.03	0.06	0.03
16	0.06	0.03	0.13	0.03	0.03	0.01	0.09	0.03	0.09	0.03
17	0.08	0.04	0.17	0.04	0.04	0.02	0.12	0.04	0.12	0.04
18	0.10	0.04	0.21	0.05	0.04	0.02	0.14	0.04	0.14	0.04
19	0.11	0.05	0.24	0.05	0.05	0.02	0.15	0.04	0.15	0.04
20	0.11	0.05	0.27	0.06	0.05	0.02	0.16	0.04	0.16	0.04
21	0.12	0.04	0.30	0.07	0.05	0.02	0.16	0.04	0.16	0.04
22	0.12	0.04	0.33	0.07	0.05	0.03	0.16	0.04	0.16	0.04
23	0.13	0.04	0.35	0.08	0.05	0.03	0.17	0.04	0.17	0.04
24	0.13	0.05	0.36	0.09	0.06	0.03	0.18	0.04	0.18	0.04
25	0.14	0.05	0.37	0.10	0.06	0.02	0.19	0.05	0.19	0.05

Table F.2 (continued)

Age	White Non-Hispanics		Black Non-Hispanics		Asian/Pacific Islanders		Mexicans		Other Hispanics	
	Men	Women	Men	Women	Men	Women	Men	Women	Men	Women
26	0.14	0.05	0.37	0.11	0.07	0.02	0.20	0.05	0.20	0.05
27	0.14	0.05	0.38	0.12	0.07	0.02	0.21	0.06	0.21	0.06
28	0.15	0.06	0.39	0.13	0.07	0.02	0.22	0.06	0.22	0.06
29	0.15	0.06	0.40	0.13	0.08	0.02	0.23	0.06	0.23	0.06
30	0.16	0.06	0.41	0.14	0.08	0.03	0.24	0.07	0.24	0.07
31	0.17	0.06	0.42	0.14	0.08	0.03	0.25	0.07	0.25	0.07
32	0.18	0.07	0.44	0.15	0.09	0.04	0.26	0.07	0.26	0.07
33	0.19	0.07	0.46	0.16	0.09	0.04	0.27	0.08	0.27	0.08
34	0.20	0.07	0.50	0.18	0.09	0.05	0.28	0.08	0.28	0.08
35	0.21	0.08	0.55	0.21	0.09	0.05	0.30	0.08	0.30	0.08
36	0.22	0.08	0.60	0.24	0.09	0.05	0.31	0.09	0.31	0.09
37	0.23	0.09	0.65	0.26	0.10	0.05	0.32	0.09	0.32	0.09
38	0.25	0.09	0.70	0.29	0.10	0.05	0.34	0.10	0.34	0.10
39	0.26	0.10	0.76	0.31	0.10	0.06	0.35	0.10	0.35	0.10
40	0.27	0.11	0.80	0.33	0.10	0.06	0.37	0.11	0.37	0.11
41	0.28	0.11	0.86	0.35	0.10	0.07	0.40	0.12	0.40	0.12
42	0.29	0.12	0.91	0.37	0.11	0.08	0.42	0.13	0.42	0.13
43	0.31	0.13	0.96	0.39	0.11	0.08	0.43	0.14	0.43	0.14
44	0.33	0.15	0.99	0.42	0.13	0.09	0.43	0.15	0.43	0.15
45	0.35	0.16	1.01	0.44	0.14	0.10	0.43	0.16	0.43	0.16
46	0.37	0.18	1.03	0.46	0.16	0.11	0.42	0.17	0.42	0.17
47	0.40	0.20	1.06	0.49	0.18	0.12	0.42	0.18	0.42	0.18
48	0.43	0.22	1.09	0.53	0.20	0.12	0.43	0.20	0.43	0.20
49	0.46	0.24	1.14	0.57	0.22	0.13	0.47	0.22	0.47	0.22
50	0.49	0.26	1.19	0.63	0.25	0.13	0.52	0.25	0.52	0.25

Table F.2 (continued)

Age	White Non-Hispanics		Black Non-Hispanics		Asian/Pacific Islanders		Mexicans		Other Hispanics	
	Men	Women	Men	Women	Men	Women	Men	Women	Men	Women
51	0.52	0.29	1.25	0.70	0.28	0.13	0.58	0.28	0.58	0.28
52	0.56	0.32	1.32	0.76	0.31	0.13	0.65	0.31	0.65	0.31
53	0.61	0.35	1.40	0.82	0.35	0.15	0.70	0.34	0.70	0.34
54	0.66	0.38	1.51	0.87	0.38	0.20	0.73	0.36	0.73	0.36
55	0.72	0.42	1.63	0.91	0.41	0.26	0.75	0.39	0.75	0.39
56	0.78	0.46	1.77	0.95	0.45	0.34	0.76	0.41	0.76	0.39
57	0.85	0.50	1.91	1.00	0.49	0.40	0.79	0.44	0.79	0.41
58	0.94	0.55	2.06	1.06	0.54	0.46	0.85	0.48	0.85	0.44
59	1.05	0.62	2.21	1.14	0.61	0.48	0.93	0.53	0.93	0.48
60	1.18	0.70	2.37	1.23	0.69	0.49	1.04	0.58	1.04	0.53
61	1.32	0.78	2.54	1.32	0.79	0.50	1.17	0.64	1.17	0.58
62	1.47	0.87	2.73	1.42	0.89	0.52	1.30	0.70	1.30	0.64
63	1.63	0.96	2.91	1.54	0.97	0.54	1.41	0.77	1.41	0.70
64	1.81	1.05	3.10	1.70	1.04	0.58	1.51	0.84	1.51	0.77
65	1.99	1.14	3.29	1.87	1.09	0.63	1.59	0.92	1.59	0.84
66	2.18	1.24	3.48	2.06	1.14	0.68	1.68	1.00	1.68	0.92
67	2.39	1.35	3.69	2.26	1.21	0.74	1.78	1.09	1.78	1.00
68	2.61	1.47	3.94	2.44	1.33	0.81	1.90	1.18	1.90	1.09
69	2.82	1.61	4.25	2.60	1.52	0.88	2.04	1.29	2.04	1.18
70	3.04	1.75	4.61	2.73	1.76	0.96	2.21	1.41	2.21	1.29
71	3.26	1.92	5.01	2.87	2.02	1.05	2.40	1.54	2.40	1.41
72	3.51	2.09	5.43	3.02	2.29	1.16	2.59	1.68	2.59	1.54
73	3.80	2.28	5.84	3.20	2.59	1.29	2.81	1.81	2.81	1.68
74	4.16	2.50	6.20	3.41	2.91	1.47	3.05	1.94	3.05	1.81
75	4.56	2.74	6.53	3.67	3.25	1.68	3.32	2.07	3.32	1.94

Table F.2 (continued)

Age	White Non-Hispanics		Black Non-Hispanics		Asian/Pacific Islanders		Mexicans		Other Hispanics	
	Men	Women	Men	Women	Men	Women	Men	Women	Men	Women
76	5.01	3.00	6.84	3.94	3.64	1.92	3.60	2.21	3.60	2.21
77	5.50	3.28	7.19	4.23	4.06	2.17	3.91	2.37	3.91	2.37
78	6.02	3.61	7.59	4.56	4.45	2.42	4.25	2.57	4.25	2.57
79	6.58	3.98	8.08	4.94	4.79	2.68	4.64	2.81	4.64	2.81
80	7.19	4.40	8.66	5.37	5.09	2.94	5.06	3.10	5.06	3.10
81	7.86	4.85	9.32	5.85	5.34	3.20	5.53	3.41	5.53	3.41
82	8.60	5.34	10.03	6.37	5.65	3.49	6.03	3.75	6.03	3.75
83	9.43	5.92	10.76	6.91	6.12	3.88	6.58	4.17	6.58	4.17
84	10.34	6.64	11.48	7.46	6.88	4.40	7.17	4.70	7.17	4.70
85	11.36	7.48	12.18	8.03	7.91	5.05	7.82	5.33	7.82	5.33
86	12.58	8.47	12.93	8.64	9.20	5.80	8.55	6.05	8.55	6.05
87	14.00	9.57	13.76	9.32	10.63	6.59	9.36	6.82	9.36	6.82
88	15.49	10.72	14.62	10.08	12.01	7.38	10.19	7.63	10.19	7.63
89	16.91	11.84	15.49	10.94	13.11	8.09	10.97	8.42	10.97	8.42
90	18.20	12.94	16.37	11.91	13.89	8.76	11.71	9.23	11.71	9.23
91	19.41	14.19	17.18	13.06	14.49	9.45	12.46	10.13	12.46	10.13
92	20.67	15.66	17.94	14.38	15.14	10.24	13.29	11.15	13.29	11.15
93	22.00	17.26	18.76	15.82	15.80	11.09	14.21	12.26	14.21	12.26
94	23.66	18.94	19.85	17.29	16.63	12.04	15.30	13.43	15.30	13.43
95	25.76	20.69	21.31	18.79	17.69	13.11	16.58	14.68	16.58	14.68
96	27.82	22.48	23.08	20.43	18.68	14.33	18.09	16.12	18.09	16.12
97	29.31	24.41	25.02	22.32	19.42	15.71	19.82	17.82	19.82	17.82
98	30.60	26.56	27.23	24.42	20.19	17.21	21.73	19.66	21.73	19.66
99	32.36	29.23	29.59	26.72	21.26	18.76	23.71	21.56	23.71	21.56
100	35.33	32.66	31.91	29.17	22.76	20.36	25.66	23.45	25.66	23.45

Table F.3

Annual Immigration by Age, Ethnicity, and Gender

a. White Non-Hispanics, Black Non-Hispanics, and Asian/Pacific Islanders, Age 0–25 Years

Age	White Non-Hispanics			Black Non-Hispanics			Asian/Pacific Islanders		
	Men	Women	Total	Men	Women	Total	Men	Women	Total
0	1,024	1,968	2,992	2,034	1,279	3,313	2,946	2,696	5,642
1	1,699	2,487	4,186	686	1,171	1,857	3,785	3,329	7,113
2	1,881	1,525	3,406	748	669	1,416	2,105	2,718	4,824
3	1,525	1,713	3,237	661	515	1,176	2,129	2,304	4,432
4	1,161	1,103	2,263	243	360	604	1,370	2,121	3,491
5	1,200	1,068	2,268	351	302	653	1,823	1,864	3,687
6	1,213	1,176	2,389	333	300	632	1,782	1,807	3,588
7	1,071	1,260	2,331	341	294	635	1,467	1,668	3,135
8	1,150	859	2,009	587	582	1,169	1,617	1,730	3,347
9	1,128	916	2,044	339	541	880	1,764	1,817	3,581
10	954	1,001	1,955	333	517	849	1,719	1,444	3,163
11	1,092	717	1,809	369	337	706	1,776	1,763	3,539
12	1,149	814	1,964	440	561	1,001	1,959	1,536	3,495
13	1,053	859	1,912	309	323	632	1,214	1,424	2,639
14	1,078	1,201	2,280	267	515	782	1,594	1,807	3,401
15	1,302	998	2,300	284	317	601	1,512	1,772	3,284
16	1,019	1,267	2,286	400	379	779	2,013	1,944	3,957
17	1,367	1,418	2,784	468	503	971	1,959	1,971	3,930
18	1,727	1,621	3,348	951	495	1,445	2,542	2,553	5,095
19	1,895	1,574	3,469	646	796	1,442	3,016	2,087	5,103
20	2,113	2,629	4,741	835	730	1,565	3,817	3,043	6,860
21	2,253	2,371	4,624	745	682	1,428	3,763	3,800	7,562
22	2,238	1,871	4,110	650	565	1,216	3,201	3,589	6,790
23	2,479	2,298	4,777	846	543	1,389	3,177	3,519	6,696
24	2,534	2,668	5,202	795	925	1,720	3,297	3,971	7,267
25	3,123	3,145	6,268	932	760	1,692	3,839	4,608	8,447

Table F.3

Annual Immigration by Age, Ethnicity, and Gender

b. Mexicans, Other Hispanics, and All Groups, Age 0–25 Years

Age	Mexicans			Other Hispanics			All Groups		
	Men	Women	Total	Men	Women	Total	Men	Women	Total
0	7,038	5,182	12,220	2,007	1,996	4,003	15,049	13,121	28,170
1	5,313	5,780	11,093	1,949	2,953	4,903	13,433	15,719	29,152
2	4,845	4,452	9,297	2,120	1,782	3,902	11,699	11,147	22,846
3	4,156	3,851	8,007	1,627	1,217	2,845	10,098	9,599	19,697
4	2,599	2,371	4,970	1,119	937	2,056	6,492	6,892	13,384
5	2,663	2,379	5,041	1,327	1,434	2,761	7,364	7,047	14,411
6	1,991	2,084	4,075	1,118	1,119	2,237	6,436	6,486	12,922
7	1,994	2,081	4,076	1,236	1,084	2,320	6,109	6,388	12,497
8	2,023	1,725	3,749	1,231	1,206	2,437	6,607	6,102	12,710
9	1,701	1,682	3,383	1,232	1,262	2,494	6,163	6,218	12,382
10	1,989	1,899	3,888	906	993	1,899	5,901	5,853	11,754
11	1,840	1,520	3,360	1,420	1,149	2,569	6,497	5,486	11,983
12	1,826	1,318	3,144	1,150	1,351	2,501	6,525	5,581	12,105
13	1,523	1,648	3,171	1,591	1,070	2,661	5,690	5,325	11,015
14	1,508	1,874	3,382	1,606	846	2,452	6,053	6,243	12,296
15	2,329	2,203	4,533	1,445	1,286	2,731	6,873	6,576	13,449
16	3,048	2,269	5,317	1,642	1,769	3,411	8,122	7,627	15,750
17	4,671	2,925	7,595	1,703	1,517	3,220	10,168	8,332	18,500
18	6,601	3,865	10,467	2,492	1,784	4,276	14,313	10,318	24,631
19	6,958	4,303	11,261	2,750	2,123	4,873	15,265	10,883	26,148
20	7,739	4,561	12,300	3,194	2,401	5,595	17,698	13,364	31,062
21	7,599	4,677	12,276	2,629	2,223	4,851	16,989	13,753	30,741
22	6,694	4,948	11,642	3,364	2,859	6,223	16,147	13,832	29,980
23	5,620	4,187	9,807	2,910	2,939	5,849	15,032	13,486	28,518
24	4,852	4,060	8,913	2,412	2,520	4,931	13,890	14,143	28,033
25	4,935	3,879	8,813	3,150	2,834	5,984	15,979	15,225	31,203

Table F.3 (continued)

c. White Non-Hispanics, Black Non-Hispanics, and Asian/Pacific Islanders, Age 26–50 Years

Age	White Non-Hispanics			Black Non-Hispanics			Asian/Pacific Islanders		
	Men	Women	Total	Men	Women	Total	Men	Women	Total
26	3,349	2,743	6,092	887	1,051	1,938	3,833	5,486	9,319
27	3,010	3,225	6,235	985	1,123	2,108	4,430	5,560	9,990
28	2,557	2,595	5,152	1,033	402	1,435	3,759	5,054	8,813
29	3,166	2,543	5,709	732	692	1,424	3,709	5,295	9,003
30	3,043	2,636	5,679	829	874	1,703	3,950	4,311	8,261
31	2,147	1,894	4,041	660	657	1,317	3,148	3,524	6,672
32	3,096	2,315	5,411	693	329	1,021	2,750	3,861	6,611
33	1,855	1,569	3,424	423	285	708	2,856	3,133	5,989
34	1,872	1,607	3,478	487	583	1,069	2,759	2,780	5,539
35	2,149	1,754	3,903	425	333	758	3,071	2,549	5,620
36	1,620	1,651	3,271	203	247	450	2,301	2,579	4,880
37	1,825	1,960	3,785	325	183	508	1,864	2,098	3,962
38	2,155	1,612	3,767	398	109	507	1,681	1,859	3,541
39	1,452	1,540	2,991	349	113	462	1,781	1,957	3,738
40	1,942	1,502	3,444	323	338	661	1,949	2,102	4,051
41	826	1,301	2,127	254	257	511	1,679	1,666	3,345
42	1,416	1,230	2,646	245	187	432	1,696	1,161	2,857
43	1,194	1,414	2,607	385	121	506	1,474	1,381	2,855
44	1,059	615	1,673	110	91	202	1,157	1,110	2,267
45	1,161	1,001	2,161	297	116	412	864	1,225	2,089
46	760	573	1,333	104	152	256	1,026	778	1,803
47	801	666	1,467	155	97	253	837	965	1,801
48	497	530	1,027	145	97	242	726	811	1,537
49	619	403	1,023	147	59	206	947	744	1,691
50	764	583	1,347	276	71	347	788	1,193	1,981

Table F.3 (continued)

d. Mexicans, Other Hispanics, and All Groups, Age 26–50 Years

Age	Mexicans			Other Hispanics			All Groups		
	Men	Women	Total	Men	Women	Total	Men	Women	Total
26	3,770	2,981	6,751	2,406	2,534	4,940	14,245	14,795	29,040
27	3,474	2,894	6,368	2,839	2,620	5,459	14,738	15,422	30,159
28	3,198	2,538	5,736	2,606	2,027	4,633	13,151	12,617	25,768
29	2,741	2,315	5,056	2,286	1,861	4,147	12,633	12,707	25,340
30	3,085	2,606	5,691	2,469	2,333	4,802	13,375	12,760	26,135
31	1,719	1,253	2,972	1,732	1,835	3,567	9,406	9,163	18,569
32	1,611	1,726	3,337	1,823	1,727	3,549	9,972	9,957	19,929
33	1,929	1,299	3,228	1,629	977	2,607	8,692	7,263	15,955
34	1,377	1,149	2,526	1,375	1,590	2,965	7,869	7,709	15,578
35	1,481	1,238	2,719	1,007	1,299	2,305	8,133	7,173	15,305
36	1,075	753	1,827	1,295	1,460	2,755	6,493	6,689	13,182
37	977	778	1,755	953	893	1,846	5,944	5,913	11,857
38	942	747	1,689	958	978	1,936	6,135	5,305	11,440
39	601	724	1,325	896	907	1,803	5,079	5,240	10,319
40	1,174	472	1,646	1,243	808	2,052	6,631	5,222	11,853
41	624	543	1,167	589	757	1,347	3,971	4,525	8,496
42	746	505	1,252	1,105	810	1,915	5,208	3,893	9,101
43	813	511	1,323	517	724	1,241	4,383	4,150	8,533
44	471	432	903	586	519	1,105	3,383	2,768	6,151
45	616	569	1,185	513	510	1,023	3,450	3,420	6,870
46	451	551	1,003	587	338	925	2,928	2,392	5,320
47	390	373	763	281	583	864	2,464	2,685	5,149
48	680	512	1,192	456	240	696	2,503	2,190	4,693
49	241	196	437	218	373	591	2,173	1,775	3,948
50	357	451	808	371	542	913	2,555	2,842	5,396

Table F.3 (continued)

e. White Non-Hispanics, Black Non-Hispanics, and Asian/Pacific Islanders, Age 51–75+ Years

Age	White Non-Hispanics			Black Non-Hispanics			Asian/Pacific Islanders		
	Men	Women	Total	Men	Women	Total	Men	Women	Total
51	389	550	939	57	0	57	832	468	1,301
52	855	839	1,694	7	67	74	431	668	1,100
53	554	413	968	116	56	171	766	893	1,659
54	449	323	772	81	0	81	555	1,211	1,767
55	350	518	868	7	211	218	598	639	1,237
56	565	253	818	30	160	190	470	785	1,255
57	379	411	791	15	110	126	559	757	1,316
58	388	656	1,043	51	110	161	701	771	1,472
59	182	572	754	90	40	130	602	807	1,409
60	376	425	801	73	47	120	599	856	1,455
61	164	491	655	0	73	73	524	769	1,293
62	225	612	837	70	16	86	444	810	1,254
63	466	246	712	0	94	94	462	640	1,102
64	300	308	608	119	37	156	449	643	1,092
65	193	399	592	40	129	169	631	772	1,403
66	278	264	541	66	104	170	401	594	995
67	252	401	653	0	90	90	509	555	1,065
68	191	396	587	26	138	164	470	550	1,020
69	471	261	733	7	37	45	281	459	740
70	139	270	410	10	66	76	425	738	1,163
71	193	224	417	17	33	50	398	185	583
72	96	210	306	37	37	74	377	341	718
73	109	223	332	16	56	71	172	316	488
74	104	131	235	0	0	0	224	188	413
75+	859	2,035	2,895	199	133	331	731	1,394	2,125
Total	93,287	91,417	184,703	27,592	25,371	52,963	128,829	142,878	271,707

Table F.3 (continued)

f. Mexicans, Other Hispanics, and All Groups, Age 51–75+ Years

Age	Mexicans			Other Hispanics			All Groups		
	Men	Women	Total	Men	Women	Total	Men	Women	Total
51	265	210	475	357	412	769	1,899	1,641	3,540
52	222	449	670	312	388	700	1,827	2,411	4,237
53	293	170	463	325	505	829	2,054	2,037	4,091
54	179	162	341	222	267	489	1,486	1,964	3,450
55	206	296	502	363	363	726	1,523	2,027	3,551
56	322	198	520	201	342	543	1,588	1,737	3,325
57	159	169	329	176	176	352	1,289	1,624	2,913
58	144	220	364	265	401	666	1,550	2,157	3,707
59	79	141	220	127	605	732	1,080	2,166	3,246
60	103	254	357	141	673	815	1,293	2,255	3,548
61	69	113	181	117	282	400	874	1,728	2,602
62	69	354	423	329	325	653	1,137	2,116	3,253
63	90	160	250	240	317	557	1,259	1,457	2,716
64	39	187	226	155	119	275	1,061	1,296	2,357
65	180	120	300	85	198	283	1,128	1,618	2,746
66	90	212	302	75	132	207	910	1,306	2,215
67	60	115	175	197	197	394	1,018	1,359	2,377
68	124	73	197	40	229	269	851	1,386	2,236
69	33	104	137	83	167	250	876	1,028	1,904
70	91	90	181	82	179	262	748	1,343	2,091
71	6	33	39	123	108	231	738	583	1,321
72	42	53	95	31	179	210	583	819	1,402
73	27	61	88	56	163	219	380	819	1,199
74	53	25	78	145	131	276	527	475	1,002
75+	264	508	772	459	793	1,252	2,512	4,863	7,375
Total	141,809	114,319	256,128	84,776	81,552	166,328	476,293	455,536	931,830

Table F.4

Annual Immigration by Age, Gender, and Education upon Arrival in United States

Age	Enrolled in Postelementary Education			Not in High School, College, or Graduate School					Total
	High School	College	Graduate School	Completed 8th Grade or Less[a]	Completed Some High School	High School Graduate	Completed Some College[b]	Received Bachelor's Degree or More	
Men									
0-14	4,577	0	0	115,452	87	0	0	0	120,115
15-17	17,699	894	0	3,876	1,905	683	106	0	25,163
18-24	11,623	25,541	4,440	27,307	13,014	18,569	6,425	2,416	109,335
25+	3,366	13,493	19,223	50,254	14,700	42,384	25,446	52,815	221,681
Total	37,264	39,928	23,663	196,889	29,705	61,636	31,977	55,232	476,293
Women									
0-14	4,505	0	0	112,598	104	0	0	0	117,207
15-17	16,703	581	0	2,755	1,757	725	14	0	22,536
18-24	9,069	20,553	3,826	17,989	8,721	18,527	7,115	3,978	89,779
25+	3,596	12,994	11,643	56,539	16,076	51,045	29,466	44,655	226,014
Total	33,873	34,128	15,469	189,882	26,659	70,297	36,596	48,633	455,536
Total									
0-14	9,081	0	0	228,050	191	0	0	0	237,322
15-17	34,402	1,475	0	6,631	3,662	1,408	120	0	47,699
18-24	20,692	46,094	8,266	45,296	21,735	37,096	13,540	6,394	199,113
25+	6,962	26,487	30,866	106,793	30,775	93,429	54,912	97,470	447,695
Total	71,138	74,056	39,132	386,770	56,364	131,933	68,572	103,865	931,830

NOTE: Totals are affected by rounding.

[a]Includes those enrolled in K–8 and those out of school who have an eighth-grade education or less.

[b]Includes associate degrees.

EDUCATION COST ESTIMATES

The RAND Education Simulation Model traces student flows into and out of the various grades in high school, college, and graduate school. To facilitate analysis of the cost of postelementary educational services, these grades were aggregated into four education levels: high school (grades 9 through 12), lower-division college (freshmen and sophomores), upper-division college (juniors and seniors), and all graduate school years.

Table G.1 displays the average annual cost estimates used in the analysis for the four aggregate education levels. The estimates are expressed in 1997 dollars, as are all cost and benefit estimates in this analysis, and include both annual operating cost and annualized capital cost.

Summing the two kinds of costs, the estimates give the total average cost per year per full-time equivalent (FTE) student at each of the

Table G.1

**Average Costs per FTE by Level of Postelementary Education
(1997 dollars)**

Education Level	Annual Operating Cost per FTE	Annualized Capital Cost per FTE	Complete Annual Cost per FTE
High school	5,983	897	6,880
Lower-division college	4,454	1,048	5,502
Upper-division college	13,143	2,078	15,221
Graduate school	20,269	3,345	23,614

SOURCE: Tables G.2 through G.5.

four education levels. The estimates are based on data for public education in California. We assume that the estimates by education level apply to private schools in California as well. Furthermore, we assume that the California cost factors apply to the rest of the nation. Limitations affecting these estimates are discussed in Chapter Three.

Tables G.2 and G.3 show our estimates of average annual operating costs and describe how they were derived from published sources; Tables G.4 and G.5 do the same for capital costs.

Table G.2 shows the average cost estimates per FTE by type of public postelementary institution in California developed by Krop, Carroll, and Ross (1995) and Shires (1996). Table G.3 allocates the undergraduate costs to lower and upper divisions by weighting the average costs by type of institution with their respective FTE enrollment. Table G.1 incorporates these estimates into the full-cost estimates needed by the model.

Table G.4 shows the cost estimates of the average annualized cost of capital per FTE by type of public postelementary institution in California developed by Shires (1996). Table G.5 allocates the undergraduate costs to lower and upper divisions in the same way as was done for operating cost. Table G.1 shows the final average operating

Table G.2

Estimated Average Annual Operating Cost of Postelementary Education

		Undergraduate Cost			
Item	High School Cost	California Community College (CCC)	California State University (CSU)	University of California (UC)	Graduate Cost at UC
Cost per FTE in 1993 $	5,353	2,906	8,868	18,135	18,135
CPI-U factor, 1993 to 1997	1.118	1.118	1.118	1.118	1.118
Cost per FTE in 1997 $	5,983	3,248	9,911	20,269	20,269

SOURCES: High school cost per FTE estimated by K–12 cost per pupil from Krop, Carroll, and Ross, 1995, p. xii. College and graduate school costs from Shires, 1996, p. 113. UC undergraduate and graduate school costs judged to be approximately the same, so estimated by the total UC cost divided by the sum of undergraduate and graduate FTEs (see Shires, 1996, p. 112).

NOTE: CPI-U factor converts 1993 dollars to 1997 dollars.

and capital cost estimates used in the RAND Education Simulation Model. These costs are exogenous to the model, i.e., are themselves a policy variable, and can be altered as appropriate.

Table G.3

Allocation of Average Undergraduate Costs per FTE to Lower and Upper Divisions: Annual Operating Cost (1997 dollars)

Education Level	California Community College (CCC)	California State University (CSU)	University of California (UC)	Total
FTE Students				
All	891,677	218,529	115,765	1,225,971
Lower division	891,677	64,288	45,795	1,001,760
Upper division	0	154,241	69,970	224,211
Total Annual Operating Cost (millions of dollars)				
All	2,896	2,166	2,346	7,408
Lower division	2,896	637	928	4,461
Upper division	0	1,529	1,418	2,947
Annual Operating Cost per FTE				
All	3,248	9,911	20,269	6,043
Lower division	3,248	9,911	20,269	4,454
Upper division	NA	9,911	20,269	13,143

SOURCES: FTE count in 1996 for CCC from Shires, 1996, p. 99. FTE counts in 1996 for CSU and UC, by lower and upper division, from Governor, State of California, *Governor's Budget Summary 1997–98* (USC counts, p. E-59; UC counts, p. E-39). Cost per FTE by type of college from Table G.2.

NOTE: By type of college (CCC, CSU, and UC), total cost estimated as FTE times cost per FTE. However, across all three types (right-side column, to get the overall lower- vs. upper-division distinction needed by the analysis), cost per FTE estimated by total cost divided by FTE.

Table G.4

Estimated Average Annualized Capital Cost per FTE of Postelementary Education

		Undergraduate Cost			
Item	High School Cost	California Community College (CCC)	California State University (CSU)	University of California (UC)	Graduate Cost at UC
Capital cost per FTE in 1993 $	15,894	15,894	26,615	59,238	59,238
Annual amortization factor	0.05052	0.05052	0.05052	0.05052	0.05052
CPI-U factor, 1993 to 1997	1.118	1.118	1.118	1.118	1.118
Annualized cost per FTE in 1997 $	897	897	1,503	3,345	3,345

SOURCES: High school capital cost per FTE assumed to be the same as for CCCs. College and graduate school capital costs per FTE from Shires, 1996, p. 116. UC undergraduate and graduate school costs judged to be approximately the same, so estimated by the total UC cost divided by the sum of undergraduate and graduate FTEs (see Shires, 1996, p. 112).

NOTES: Annualized capital cost assumes 40-year expected facility life and 4 percent real discount rate. CPI-U factor converts 1993 dollars to 1997 dollars.

Table G.5

Allocation of Average Undergraduate Costs per FTE to Lower and Upper Divisions: Annualized Capital Cost
(1997 dollars)

Education Level	California Community College (CCC)	California State University (CSU)	University of California (UC)	Total
FTE Students				
All	891,677	218,529	115,765	1,225,971
Lower division	891,677	64,288	45,795	1,001,760
Upper division	0	154,241	69,970	224,211
Total Annualized Cost of Capital (millions of dollars)				
All	800	328	387	1,516
Lower division	800	97	153	1,050
Upper division	0	232	234	466
Annualized Cost of Capital per FTE				
All	897	1,503	3,345	1,237
Lower division	897	1,503	3,345	1,048
Upper division	NA	1,503	3,345	2,078

SOURCES: FTE count in 1996 for CCC from Shires, 1996, p. 99. FTE counts in 1996 for CSU and UC, by lower and upper division, from Governor, State of California, *Governor's Budget Summary 1997–98* (USC counts, p. E-59; UC counts, p. E-39). Cost per FTE by type of college from Table G.4.

NOTE: By type of college (CCC, CSU, and UC), total cost estimated as FTE times cost per FTE. However, across all three types (right-side column, to get the overall lower- vs. upper-division distinction needed by the analysis), cost per FTE estimated by total cost divided by FTE.

ADULT POPULATION IN 1990 AND PROJECTED
TO 2015

Table H.1 compares the estimated (1990) and projected (2015) number of adults age 25 or older by ethnicity, nativity, and level of education in both California and the rest of the nation. These figures are the basis for all figures and tables in Chapter Four.

Table H.1

Adult Population Age 25 or Older, 1990 and 2015, by Ethnicity, Nativity, Education, and Location

	California		Rest of Nation	
Nativity/Education	1990	2015	1990	2015
	Asians			
Native-born				
Not high school grad	26,602	34,182	77,750	63,443
High school grad	60,183	123,109	142,710	334,690
Some college	98,841	339,546	136,530	475,128
College grad	120,813	433,060	146,025	490,418
Subtotal	306,439	929,897	503,015	1,363,679
Immigrant				
Not high school grad	334,875	499,132	456,290	653,921
High school grad	214,834	595,371	316,505	910,026
Some college	318,041	930,643	349,080	1,120,402
College grad	441,155	1,516,800	816,500	2,385,874
Subtotal	1,308,905	3,541,946	1,938,375	5,070,223
Total	1,615,344	4,471,843	2,441,390	6,433,902

Table H.1 (continued)

Nativity/Education	California		Rest of Nation	
	1990	2015	1990	2015
Blacks				
Native-born				
Not high school grad	271,374	140,344	5,266,605	3,117,480
High school grad	274,339	470,998	3,965,910	7,141,594
Some college	415,737	644,130	3,087,570	5,656,452
College grad	162,940	259,209	1,462,270	2,670,900
Subtotal	1,124,390	1,514,681	13,782,355	18,586,426
Immigrant				
Not high school grad	9,880	13,114	239,830	232,556
High school grad	9,947	31,395	195,230	492,956
Some college	20,148	46,665	219,020	477,098
College grad	13,574	30,315	159,635	352,923
Subtotal	53,549	121,489	813,715	1,555,533
Total	1,177,939	1,636,170	14,596,070	20,141,959
Mexicans				
Native-born				
Not high school grad	432,083	588,421	902,095	1,175,715
High school grad	339,697	1,159,668	636,680	1,685,289
Some college	341,891	1,114,054	485,225	1,308,949
College grad	103,127	309,961	190,850	504,461
Subtotal	1,216,798	3,172,104	2,214,850	4,674,414
Immigrant				
Not high school grad	1,230,260	2,517,171	976,195	1,857,827
High school grad	189,791	1,077,674	154,870	718,295
Some college	158,118	757,989	116,160	451,825
College grad	50,148	248,104	53,865	206,969
Subtotal	1,628,317	4,600,938	1,301,090	3,234,916
Total	2,845,115	7,773,042	3,515,940	7,909,330
Other Hispanics				
Native-born				
Not high school grad	127,265	72,690	1,321,060	963,265
High school grad	154,298	171,997	1,451,580	1,192,138
Some college	193,528	241,667	1,041,925	1,036,553
College grad	105,063	120,236	666,750	650,833
Subtotal	580,154	606,590	4,481,315	3,842,789
Immigrant				
Not high school grad	346,825	536,782	1,527,205	1,261,521
High school grad	127,465	331,780	693,235	1,101,754
Some college	147,543	342,071	590,510	858,476
College grad	84,790	202,240	404,200	721,467
Subtotal	706,623	1,412,873	3,215,150	3,943,218
Total	1,286,777	2,019,463	7,696,465	7,786,007

Table H.1 (continued)

Nativity/Education	California		Rest of Nation	
	1990	2015	1990	2015
White Non-Hispanics				
Native-born				
Not high school grad	1,397,351	615,616	22,307,940	9,284,905
High school grad	2,548,287	2,758,571	34,565,060	35,778,336
Some college	3,690,680	4,356,600	26,695,560	34,645,987
College grad	2,994,465	3,647,208	22,954,000	31,760,715
Subtotal	10,630,783	11,377,995	106,522,560	111,469,943
Immigrant				
Not high school grad	228,951	152,315	1,450,915	500,599
High school grad	213,430	308,085	1,081,730	1,263,278
Some college	270,914	435,313	840,255	1,222,060
College grad	267,060	530,636	917,860	1,751,894
Subtotal	980,355	1,426,349	4,290,760	4,737,831
Total	11,611,138	12,804,344	110,813,320	116,207,774
All Groups				
Native-born				
Not high school grad	2,254,675	1,451,253	29,875,450	14,604,808
High school grad	3,376,804	4,684,343	40,761,940	46,132,047
Some college	4,740,677	6,695,997	31,446,810	43,123,069
College grad	3,486,408	4,769,674	25,419,895	36,077,327
Immigrant				
Not high school grad	2,150,791	3,718,514	4,650,435	4,506,424
High school grad	755,467	2,344,305	2,441,570	4,486,309
Some college	914,764	2,512,681	2,115,025	4,129,861
College grad	856,727	2,528,095	2,352,060	5,419,127
Total				
Not high school grad	4,405,466	5,169,767	34,525,885	19,111,232
High school grad	4,132,271	7,028,648	43,203,510	50,618,356
Some college	5,655,441	9,208,678	33,561,835	47,252,930
College grad	4,343,135	7,297,769	27,771,955	41,496,454
Total	18,536,313	28,704,862	139,063,185	158,478,972

SOURCE: RAND Education Simulation Model.

ESTIMATES OF COSTS AND BENEFITS

Table I.1 contains the estimated increase in costs, savings in public expenditures, increase in tax revenues, and increase in individual disposable income (private benefits) associated with each of the four alternative goals we considered as possible ways to reduce the educational attainment gap for blacks and Hispanics. (See Chapter Five for discussion.) These costs and benefits are over the life of a given cohort discounted at 4 percent to 1997 dollars.

Figure I.1 displays the distribution of public benefits (savings in public expenditures and increase in tax revenues) by sources under the "full equalization" goal for both California and the rest of the nation. There are a few notable differences between the two areas in the relative importance of the various sources of public benefits.

Savings in government programs account for a larger share of public savings in the rest of the nation (48 percent) than in California (37 percent). The reason for this difference is that the savings accruing to the criminal justice system (jails and prisons) would be larger in the rest of the nation (21 percent) than in California (11 percent). In turn, this result stems from the different compositions of the minority populations in the two areas. Mexicans, who are proportionately more numerous in California than in the rest of the nation, are less likely to be incarcerated than are blacks and Other Hispanics, two groups who are proportionately more numerous in the rest of the nation. In contrast, savings in expenditures for income transfers, health care, and Social Security are similar in both areas.

The increases in FICA revenues and federal income tax revenues are sizable in both California and the rest of the nation, each accounting for more than 20 percent of the public benefits derived from the increased education of minorities. However, because California has, on the average, higher income and sales tax rates than does the rest of the nation, it would reap proportionately twice as much as the rest of the nation in additional state revenues if the "full equalization" goal were met.

Table I.1

Estimated Costs and Benefits of Meeting Alternative Education Goals
for Blacks and Hispanics, California and Rest of the Nation
(1997 dollars, billions)

| Goals | Costs | Benefits | | | |
		Savings in Public Expenditures	Income Tax Revenues	Subtotal Public Benefits	Private Benefits
California					
"High school"	1.8	1.9	2.2	4.2	3.9
"College-going"	2.7	2.4	3.3	5.7	5.9
"College retention"	0.5	.01	0.5	0.6	0.9
"Full equalization"	3.6	2.6	4.4	7.0	7.7
Rest of the Nation					
"High school"	3.7	6.6	5.3	11.9	9.1
"College-going"	4.6	7.2	6.3	13.7	11.3
"College retention"	1.0	0.3	0.9	1.2	1.6
"Full equalization"	6.1	7.6	8.2	15.8	14.0

SOURCE: RAND Education Simulation Model.

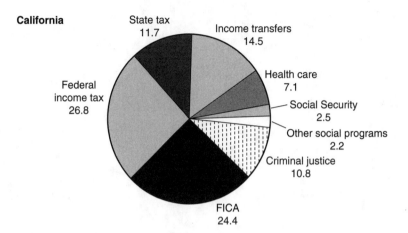

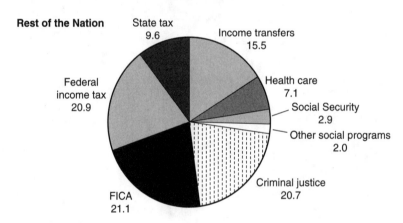

SOURCE: RAND Education Simulation Model.

NOTE: Income transfers include welfare, food stamps, SSI, and unemployment insurance; health care includes Medicaid and Medicare; and other social programs include lunch and energy programs.

Figure I.1—Sources of Public Benefits Under "Full Equalization" Goal, California and Rest of the Nation

REFERENCES

Ashenfelter, O., and A. Krueger, "Estimates of the Economic Return to Schooling from a New Sample of Twins," *Working Paper Series*, National Bureau of Economic Research Working Paper No. 4143, August 1992.

Baumol, W. J., "On the Discount Rate for Public Projects," in E. Mansfield (ed.), *Microeconomics, Selected Readings*, New York: Norton, 1979.

Blake, J., *Family Size and Achievement*, Berkeley: University of California Press, 1989.

Borjas, G. J., and L. Hilton, "Immigration and the Welfare State: Immigrant Participation in Means-Tested Entitlement Programs," *The Quarterly Journal of Economics*, May 1995.

Bowen, W. G., and D. Bok, *The Shape of the River: Long-Term Consequences of Considering Race in College and University Admissions*, Princeton, NJ: Princeton University Press, 1998.

Cohn, E., *Economics of State Aid to Education*, Lexington, MA: Lexington Books, 1974.

Commission on National Investment in Higher Education, *Breaking the Social Contract: The Fiscal Crisis in Higher Education*, New York: Council for Aid to Education, CAE-100, 1997.

Congressional Budget Office, *The Economic and Budget Outlook: Fiscal Years 1998–2007*, Washington, DC, 1997.

Cummings, Ronald G. (ed.), *Journal of Environmental Economics and Management*, Vol. 18, No. 2, Part 2, March 1990.

DaVanzo, J., et al., *Surveying Immigrant Communities: Policy Imperatives and Technical Challenges*, Santa Monica, CA: RAND, MR-247-FF, 1994.

Duan, N., et al., "A Comparison of Alternative Models for the Demand for Medical Care," *Journal of Business & Economic Statistics*, Vol. 1, No. 2, April 1983.

Economic Report of the President, Washington, DC: GPO, February 1996.

Ettinger, M. P., et al., *Who Pays? A Distributional Analysis of the Tax Systems in All 50 States*, Washington, DC: Citizens for Tax Justice and the Institute on Taxation and Economic Policy, June 1996.

Federation for American Immigration Reform, *Immigration Report*, Vol. XIV, No. 7, July 1994.

Friedman, L. S., "Chapter 3: The Specification of Individual Choice Models for the Analysis of Welfare Programs," in *Microeconomic Policy Analysis*, New York: McGraw-Hill, 1984.

Governor, State of California, *Governor's Budget Summary 1997–98*, submitted to the California Legislature, 1996–97 regular session.

Griliches, Z., "Estimating the Returns to Schooling: Some Econometric Problems," *Econometrica*, Vol. 45, No. 1, January 1977.

Grissmer, D. W., et al., *Student Achievement and the Changing American Family*, Santa Monica, CA: RAND, MR-488-LE, 1994.

Grossman, M., and L. Benham, "Health, Hours, and Wages," in M. Perlman (ed.), *The Economics of Health and Medical Care*, New York: John Wiley, 1974.

Grossman, M., and R. Kaestner, "Effects of Education on Health," in Jere R. Behrman and Nevzer Stacey (eds.), *Social Benefits of Education*, Ann Arbor: University of Michigan Press, 1997.

Halfon, N., et al., "Medical Enrollment and Health Services Access by Latino Children in Inner-City Los Angeles," *The Journal of the American Medical Association*, 277, February 26, 1997.

Hanushek, E. A., "The Trade-Off Between Child Quantity and Quality," *Journal of Political Economy*, Vol. 100, 1992, pp. 84–117.

Haveman, R. and B. Wolfe, *Succeeding Generations: On the Effects of Investments in Children*, New York: Russell Sage Foundation, 1984.

Hill, M. A., and J. O'Neill, "Family Endowment and the Achievement of Young Children with Special Reference to the Underclass," unpublished mimeo, 1993.

Jaynes, G. D., "The Labor Market Status of Black Americans: 1939–1985," *Journal of Economic Perspectives*, Vol. 4, No. 1, Fall 1990, pp. 9–24.

Krop, C., S. J. Carroll, and R. L. Ross, *Tracking Education Spending in California*, Santa Monica, CA: RAND, MR-548-SFR, 1995.

Krop, R., *The Social Returns to Increased Investment in Education: Measuring the Effect of Education on the Cost of Social Programs*, RAND Graduate School Dissertation, Santa Monica, CA: RAND, RGSD-138, 1998.

Maguire, K., and A. L. Pastore (eds.), *Sourcebook of Criminal Justice Statistics—1994*, Washington, DC: U.S. Department of Justice, Bureau of Justice Statistics, 1995.

Manning, W. G., et al., *Health Insurance and the Demand for Medical Care: Evidence from a Randomized Experiment*, Santa Monica, CA: RAND, R-3476-HHS, 1987.

McCarthy, K. F., and G. Vernez, *Immigration in a Changing Economy*, Santa Monica, CA: RAND, MR-854-OSD/CBR/FF/WFHF/AMF, 1997.

Mickelson, R. A., "The Attitude-Achievement Paradox Among Black Adolescents," *Sociology of Education*, Vol. 63, 1990, pp. 44–61.

Moffitt, R., "Incentive Effects of the U.S. Welfare System: A Review," *Journal of Economic Literature*, Vol. XXX, March 1992, pp. 1–61.

National Research Council, *The New Americans: Economic, Demographic and Fiscal Effects of Immigration,* Washington, DC, 1997.

Ogbu, J. U., "Immigrant and Involuntary Minorities in Comparative Perspective," in M. A. Gibson and J. U. Ogbu (eds.), *Minority Status and Schooling: A Comparative Study of Immigrants and Involuntary Minorities,* New York and London: Garland Publishing, Inc., 1991, pp. 3–33.

Papademetriou, D. G., and S. Yale-Loehr, *Balancing Interests: Rethinking U.S. Selection of Skilled Immigrants,* Washington, DC: Carnegie Endowment for International Peace, 1996.

Pascarella, E. T., and P. T. Terenzini, *How College Affects Students,* San Francisco, CA: Jossey-Bass Publishers, 1991.

Portes, A., and R. G. Rumbaut, *Immigrant America: A Portrait,* Berkeley: University of California Press, 1996.

President's Advisory Commission on Educational Excellence for Hispanic Americans, *Our Nation on the Fault Line: Hispanic American Education,* 1996.

Psacharopoulos, G., and M. Woodhall, *Education for Development: An Analysis of Investment Choices,* England: Oxford University Press, 1985.

Rank, M. R., and L. Cheng, "Welfare Use Across Generations: How Important Are the Ties That Bind?" *Journal of Marriage and the Family,* 57, August 1995, pp. 673–684.

Schoeni, R. F., K. McCarthy, and G. Vernez, *The Mixed Economic Progress of Immigrants,* Santa Monica, CA: RAND, MR-763-IF/FF, 1996.

Shires, M. A., *The Future of Public Undergraduate Education in California,* Santa Monica, CA: RAND, MR-561-LE, 1996.

Smith, J. P., and F. Welch, *Closing the Gap: Forty Years of Economic Progress for Blacks,* Santa Monica, CA: RAND, R-3330, 1986.

Stacey, N., "Social Benefits of Education," *The Annals of the American Academy,* 559, September 1998, pp. 54–63.

Steinberg, L., *Beyond the Classroom,* New York: Simon and Schuster, 1996.

Sturm, R., *How Do Education and Training Affect a Country's Economic Performance? A Literature Review,* Santa Monica, CA: RAND, MR-197-LE, 1993.

Suarez-Orozco, M. M., and C. E. Suarez-Orozco, "The Cultural Patterning of Achievement Motivation: A Comparison of Mexican, Mexican Immigrant, Mexican American, and Non-Latino White American Students," in R. G. Rumbaut and W. A. Cornelius (eds.), *California's Immigrant Children: Theory, Research, and Implications for Educational Policy,* Center for U.S.-Mexican Studies, San Diego: University of California, 1995.

U.S. Commission on Immigration Reform, *Becoming an American: Immigration and Immigrant Policy,* Washington, DC, 1997.

U.S. Department of Health and Human Services, Health Care Financing Administration, Medicaid Bureau, *Medicaid Statistics: Program and Financial Statistics Fiscal Year 1992,* Washington, DC, 1993.

U.S. Department of the Treasury, Internal Revenue Service, *Statistics of Income—1992 Individual Income Tax Returns,* Washington, DC, 1995.

U.S. House of Representatives, Committee on Ways and Means, *1996 Green Book: Background Material and Data on Programs Within the Jurisdiction of the Committee on Ways and Means,* Washington, DC: GPO, 1996.

Vernez, G., *Immigrant Women in the United States Labor Force,* Lanham, Maryland: Lexington Books, 1999.

Vernez, G., and A. Abrahamse, *How Immigrants Fare in U.S. Education,* Santa Monica, CA: RAND, MR-718-AMF, 1996.

Willis, R. J., "Wage Determinants: A Survey and Reinterpretation of Human Capital Earnings Functions," in Orley Ashenfelter and Richard Layard (eds.), *Handbook of Labor Economics,* Vol. I, Amsterdam: Elsevier Science Publishers BV, 1986.

Witte, A. D., "Crime," in Jere R. Behrman and Nevzer Stacey (eds.), *Social Benefits of Education*, Ann Arbor: University of Michigan Press, 1997.